Reading & Teaching

Henry Giroux

TEACHING
❧ CONTEMPORARY ❧
SCHOLARS

Joe L. Kincheloe & Shirley R. Steinberg

General Editors

Vol. 4

PETER LANG
New York • Washington, D.C./Baltimore • Bern
Frankfurt am Main • Berlin • Brussels • Vienna • Oxford

Clar Doyle & Amarjit Singh

Reading & Teaching
Henry Giroux

PETER LANG
New York • Washington, D.C./Baltimore • Bern
Frankfurt am Main • Berlin • Brussels • Vienna • Oxford

Library of Congress Cataloging-in-Publication Data

Doyle, Clar.
Reading and teaching Henry Giroux / Clar Doyle, Amarjit Singh.
p. cm. — (Teaching contemporary scholars; vol. 4)
Includes bibliographical references and index.
1. Critical pedagogy. 2. Giroux, Henry A.
I. Singh, Amarjit. II. Title.
LC196.D695   370.11'5—dc22   2006019574
ISBN 978-0-8204-8175-3
ISSN 1533-4082

Bibliographic information published by **Die Deutsche Bibliothek**.
Die Deutsche Bibliothek lists this publication in the "Deutsche
Nationalbibliografie"; detailed bibliographic data is available
on the Internet at http://dnb.ddb.de/.

Cover design by Lisa Barfield

The paper in this book meets the guidelines for permanence and durability
of the Committee on Production Guidelines for Book Longevity
of the Council of Library Resources.

For Neera and David, and for Garrett, Ceara, and Damhnait
You remain a constant source of joy and pride.

Contents

Acknowledgments

I am grateful to all my former and current colleagues, and all the staff at the Faculty of Education, Memorial University of Newfoundland. I have appreciated greatly their warmth and love with which they have treated me for more than three decades. I am indebted also to my former and current colleagues and friends at the East West Center, Honolulu, and the University of Hawaii at Manoa. For the last three decades I have benefited greatly from their friendship, encouragement, support and knowledge of the practice of teaching multiculturalism and diversity in schools and at other public spheres. I want to express my special gratitude to Professors Tony Lenzer, Gene Kassebaum, Kiyoshi Ikeda, Eldon Wegner, Hunter McEwen, David Ericson, Larry Smith, Greg Trifonovitch and Krishna Kumar for their efforts to provide me with opportunities to carry on my work. I would like to thank professors Eileen Tamura, Gay Reed, Bill Gushue, George Hache, I.J. Baksh, Wilf Martin, Joan Oldford, Jagdish Sharma, Mimi Sharma and Mike and Judy Hamnett (unfortunately Judy is no more with us), Gord Ralph, Walter Okshevsky, Dave Dibbon, all of whom, in different ways showed me care and kindness, over the last several years. I extend heartfelt thanks to Bill, Andrea, Alice and Kevin for endless stimulating discussions on various topics. My good friends Gary and Gerry Gairola have been good conversational partners whose insightful questions always left me thinking more deeply and clearly about the concepts of diaspora and the diasporic subjects. Special thanks are also due to my dear friend and colleague Ruth Larkin for her constant support. I wish to record my debt of gratitude to Michael Cheang, Becky Goodman, Carol Matsumiya, Sharon Takara, Lucy and John Witeck, Bill and Barbara Roberts for facilitating my work in many different ways. My parents and siblings have provided me with unconditional love. I wish to thank Susie Bird and her family, Bowie Hannah and the Webbs for their help. My wife Mary Power and our son David Patrick Power Singh have been a steady source of strength and joy for me. My loving daughter Neera Ann Bird Singh and her husband Mori Cancio gave us a beautiful granddaughter, Tala Mita Singh Cancio. My in-laws, the Power clan in Newfoundland, and my daughter's and our *ohana* in Honolulu-Pono Shim, aunty Dawn and Chantelle, the extended family of Lyn and Mike, Wess, Stacy and their daughter Daniel, Sam and Jill Lankford and the kids Jordon and Jessie, Randy and Lorna Larsen and the kids Shawn and Malorie, Fred and Viki Larson and the kids Nash and Kit, Ross and Audrey Sutherland and the kids Laura and Ian, Judy and Jeff Lilly and their daughter Antoinette, and Anita and Bill Hodges provided me a sense of place as dwelling. I thank all these people for their support and attention. Their generosity provided me an invigorating sense of the dialectic nature of transnationality that has been an inspiring and humbling experience for me. Amarjit.

The Faculty of Education at Memorial University has been a place of constant reflection and renewal for me. I appreciate and enjoy our students. I am invigorated by my discussions with Ursula, Dennis, Dave, Fred and Henry. I thank my cherished friends Kim, Bill, Alice, Andrea, Kevin, Ted, Morgan, Katherine and Eileen for their warmth and the shared coffee. Nic has been there all these years and during all these journeys. I am grateful to Loretto for her continued friendship. Devlin and Finlay are ever with me. Margaret's spirit and worldview is an inspiration to us all. I thank Rosanne for her under-standing, care and support. Garrett, Ceara and Damhnait you remain that beacon of light for me. Clar.

We both thank Ceara Doyle for her dedicated work in scanning the Giroux material, Margie Moore for her careful editing and design work, Amy Chislett for her proofreading and Walter Okshevsky for his reading and thoughtful comments. Carolyn Lono and Laura Walsh, as always, were most helpful and patient. We are most grateful to Joe Kincheloe and Shirley Steinberg, the series editors, and the production team at Peter Lang.

Henry, this one's for you.

Introduction

Giroux is one of the world's leading contemporary critical, social, educational and cultural theorists. From our perspective, Giroux's writings are indispensable for those who engage in educating future teachers and democratic leaders. While his writings are complex and massive, we believe that his work needs to be read by students, teachers, and those interested in issues related to school, society, culture, and the development of democratic society. One of Giroux's main aims has been to link critical pedagogy, cultural studies, and democracy. In this way Giroux has done much to help transform both education and society. The major impetus to develop this book comes from the desire of many of our students and colleagues to integrate Giroux's understandings of critical and reflective pedagogy into their work. We have been committed to integrating Giroux's writings in our courses, teacher education programs, research activities, and cultural work for many years. We are attempting to do this in a reasonable fashion. We say reasonable because there are constraints, owing to the fact that limited class time is available, classes are large, and there are competing sets of materials that need to be included in our work in an era of downsizing, restructuring, and teacher education reform. However, we are following Giroux's lead when we say that students should be given the opportunity to read texts that affirm and interrogate their own realities.

Our experience teaches us that this is not an easy task. There are certain constraints that need to be overcome in order to achieve this goal. People find themselves in varied institutional settings. Nevertheless, we have been able to use Giroux's work in many different ways in our various pedagogical and cultural projects. We realize that we are not alone in doing such work. In this book we attempt to represent how Giroux has inspired our work over an extensive period of time. Like Giroux we are interested in a pedagogy that is inflicted with a politics of possibility and hope. As we are trying to assist students "define themselves and their relationships to the social world" we try and remind ourselves of the connections among culture, pedagogy, politics, and power. Along with our students we are part of such a nexus. (Giroux & Myrsiades, 2001, p. 7). We try to remain aware of the moral implications of our pedagogy. We realize that we have responsibilities for the "knowledge we produce, the social relations we legitimate, and the ideologies and identities we offer up to students" (Giroux, 2004, p. 119).

We have organized this book in two sections. The first section presents selections of writings that serve as a basis for our reading of Henry Giroux. In the second section, we share how we make use of those writings in our teaching, teacher education, research, and cultural work. The concept of voice is an important one for this book. In the first section we try and allow Giroux to speak through his writings. In the second section we give voice to our students and fellow cultural workers. It is not our agenda here to critique the writings of Henry Giroux. However, in the way that we have selected and used these writings, it is obvious that we do not take Giroux's work for granted or in a non-critical fashion. In particular, we wish to present a balanced agenda for our students, colleagues, and fellow cultural workers. We read, for example, that Giroux does not simply wish to tar corporations or institutions with the same brush. This is evident when he writes about capitalism in *The Terror Of Neoliberalism* (2004) or higher education in *Take Back Higher Education* (2004). Giroux claims that educators need help to "create organizations capable of mobilizing civic dialogue, provide an alternative conception of the meaning and purpose of higher education" (2000, p. 56). That, in part, is what we are trying to do. Giroux's discussion of public intellectuals and their functions in society is a significant one for us in the particular work that we do. Giroux believes that we need an expansive and political conception of the public intellectual. In particular he "focuses on the practices of educators and other cultural workers who construct, present, and engage various forms of images, texts, and actions within and outside of the university" (1997b, p. 152). This speaks directly to our agenda. In particular, Giroux stresses that the university is a sort of knowledge industry that has tremendous influence on so many people. He claims that if the university is to have any credibility as a public sphere, it must recognize that educators play a crucial role in shaping the identities, values, and beliefs of students. In short, universities, like public schools, are crucial in forming identity. In this work we try to be acutely aware of our own locations, in the social and institutional structures that we find ourselves in. We, in our daily lives as educators and cultural workers, try to be aware of the multiple locations of our students, their parents and communities, and the many other people with whom we work. Giroux suggests that we take the notion of leadership, criticism, and solidarity seriously.

We believe in trying to create conditions for students, and those we work with, that will encourage them to examine their roles as concerned citizens. In short, we are interested in a pedagogy of affirmation. In this pedagogical project, we take up Giroux's challenge and try to indicate how both teachers and students can learn from each other and become transformative educators, intellectuals, and cultural workers. To act on this challenge, we have created conditions at a number of sites including classrooms for critically reading and teaching Giroux; graduate and faculty research for the production of knowledge informed by Giroux's theoretical and pedagogical writings; community drama where cultural production is driven by and for transformative moments; and a teaching internship process for critical and reflective teacher education. In fact, this book could be seen as a site where we are attempting to frame, in our own way, a selection of Giroux's writings for praxis.

In the first part of the book, called *Reading Giroux*, we are not claiming to present his writings in a chronological fashion. Instead, we begin with a central topic and allow Giroux's thoughts about that topic to be illuminated through quotations and comments. We are also acutely aware of the limiting borders we place around any of these topics. We take pains to state that no topic can be contained within its name, or understood without reference to other topics. This approach serves our present purpose.

In the second part of the book, called *Teaching Giroux*, we present, by way of sample and example, how we have used Giroux's writings in our own work. This work covers the gamut of intellectual work from teaching university courses, work in teacher education, research, thesis supervision, and curriculum development to cultural production. This work is not offered as any sort of model, but rather as an indicator of how Giroux has influenced work in universities, public schools, and communities. We believe that Giroux's writings, along with the work of other notable educational and social theorists, have had a tremendous influence on everyday thought and action.

In the introduction to Giroux's *Pedagogy and the Politics of Hope* the series editors rightly claim that his work is prodigious and multidimensional. However, these editors do manage to put Giroux's work in quite a neat shell when they claim that his struggle for a radical democracy, "involves the effort to expand the possibility for social justice, freedom, and egalitarian social relations in the educational, economic, political, and cultural domains that locate men, women, and children in everyday life" (1997a, p. ix). There is real truth to the claim, made by Kincheloe, McLaren, and Steinberg that Giroux has been able to unmask the ways that power creeps through educational institutions in a fashion that undermines and marginalizes certain people. This claim comes from scholars who have had no small part in that unmasking. However, Giroux's work extends far beyond the relationship between power and marginalized students, to encompass many of us who work in educational and cultural sites. We believe that after Giroux we can never look at our educational relationships and institutions with the same naiveté.

As Peter McLaren acknowledges in the forward for *Teachers as Intellectuals* (1988a) it is difficult to do justice to the scope and critical depth of Henry Giroux's work. Part of our challenge, in this text, is to give some context for that body of work. We do this by indicating the macrolevels that Giroux writes about, and we offer a microcontext for working from his writings. In large part, what Giroux has offered is a critical social theory that challenges the prevailing view of schooling. Giroux's work has been groundbreaking and seminal in character. As part of the process of offering this critical social theory, Giroux has given us conceptual tools to interrogate the loaded mix of school and society. As is evident by the selection of writings presented in this present text, the mix of school and society is most complicated. One of the things that most intrigues us about Giroux is that he never tries to soften that complexity. He insists on facing head-on the difficult concept or the problematic practice. Over the time of his writings, he can be seen to be openly struggling with many of the ideas involved. He is never satisfied with the simple solution or the pat answer. He shows great respect for the ideas, as well as the people, who have to live by them. Of course, Giroux is never satisfied with simply naming and blaming. In the end, he is concerned with the empowerment of students and the transforming of the larger social order that will allow a faithful democracy. These are demanding and tangled challenges. The reality of schooling and society are such that the complexities must be acknowledged. Giroux certainly acknowledges such complexities, yet his vision is one of possibility and hope. It is within a matrix of complexity, possibility, and hope that we present and comment on some topics gleaned from Henry Giroux's writings.

In many ways Giroux's sense of hope lies in the dialectical relationship between social structure and human agency. Giroux fully realizes that individuals are both producers and products of history. He places great significance on the place of culture and power in his attempt to understand how schools and society are locked together. Giroux believes it is important that teachers and students need to appreciate that meaning is actively constructed through the many formations of lived and shared experiences. Therefore, as far as Giroux is concerned, teachers need to make students' experiences relevant, problematic, and critical. For Giroux, the notion of teacher as transformative intellectual is important because he sees teaching as an emancipatory practice.

It helps to see pedagogy as the production of attitudes, values, knowledge, and identities, which takes place in a variety of cultural and social sites. For Giroux, pedagogy is far beyond transmission. He has an aversion to legitimating an authoritarian knowledge that simply delivers prepackaged content, instructional methodologies, and assessment mechanisms. As far as Giroux is concerned, part of the pedagogical struggle is to demystify the hidden forms of domination. He has done much to help this process. Giroux believes that often it is hard for educators, working in a dominant pedagogy, to deal with the difference of culture, politics, gender and class. In fact, we often see difference equated with deviance. As far as critical pedagogy is concerned, difference is seen as absolutely central and for Giroux it is necessary to put such difference inside the curriculum. This is where Giroux calls for educators and students to be "border crossers."

One of the greatest contributions made by Giroux, from our point of view, is in the development of the concept of teachers as transformative intellectuals. This becomes a very important concept for us as we develop the second part of this book. Giroux believes it is crucial for teachers to get beyond a pedagogy of servility and bridge the normative gap between thinking and acting. We will expand on this topic, under the titles of Teachers and Curriculum, as well as in the *Teaching Giroux* part of this book. One of Giroux's expressed concerns is that teachers are becoming deskilled. Not because of any fault of theirs, but because of the way teaching is prescribed and curriculum is prepackaged. One of the most dangerous examples of this can be seen in the artificial split between curriculum development and curriculum implementation. As an experienced high school teacher, Giroux would know, only too well, how difficult it is to find time to simply implement curriculum. Still·this division of labour is problematic. As we probe Giroux's notion of teachers as transformative intellectuals, we realize that he means that they "understand the nature of their own self-formation, and have a future, see the importance of education as a public discourse, and have some sense of mission in providing students which they need to become critical citizens" (1993b, p. 15).

Giroux expands his notion of teachers as transformative intellectuals by claiming that they are also cultural workers. He realizes that it is not easy to teach others to be transformative intellectuals. However, if we are to do this we need to learn to move beyond the language of methodologies, management, and professionalism. For Giroux, the disciplines of schooling need to be examined, dismantled, and reconstructed, and it would seem that teachers need to find ways to give themselves the power to do this. Of course this is a most complex and difficult task. We believe that part of this struggle has to begin with professors of education offering, and teachers asking for, more than "how to do it" exercises, formulas, and programs.

In examining other aspects of Giroux's work, we constantly see the term "border." The terms of border and border crossing have become important in educational studies. Of course from a subject or discipline-bound view of schooling this everbecoming or homelessness is a crucial aspect of breaking down the rigid and often artificial borders placed on knowledge. In real life we are not so bound by such strict borders. For example, we often discuss the history of a country, map the geography, as well as calculate the miles and expense of travel in that country without the artificial changing of disciplinary gears. Giroux believes we have to do this in pedagogy.

Following on the lead and seminal works of Paulo Freire, Giroux has earned for himself the role as champion proponent of the critical pedagogy movement. Like others in that movement, Giroux believes that education is a central factor in determining social and political relationships. Giroux has been a prime mover in continually reworking the concepts and processes of critical pedagogy throughout these recent decades. He knows that critical pedagogy is not a set-in-concrete dogma for the ages. If critical pedagogy is to remain relevant, it too must shift its concepts and skills to integrate education and society.

In relation to education, Giroux cuts to the chase when he claims that there is a need "to name the contradiction between what schools claim they do and what they actually do" (2005a, p. 125). In other words, part of the critical pedagogy agenda is to shed much needed light on the processes of schooling. Giroux has done much to use his own laser light to expose what is happening in education, schooling, and pedagogy. It should be noted that he is as interested in telling what is positive about education, schooling, and pedagogy as he is in exposing the contradictions. Those who would claim otherwise are not reading the balance and possibility that exists in his work.

Another helpful concept for our pedagogical and cultural work has been ideology. Much of what we have learned about the power of this concept has come from Giroux. He sees ideology as part of a circle of power, and he is concerned with the material apparatus at work, as well as the text and ideology in a particular classroom. In many instances, Giroux is able to show that he can cut through the logic and unmask the ideology of new right and neoliberal democratic claims: "Within the discourse of neo-liberalism, democracy becomes synonymous with free markets while issues of equality, social justice, and freedom are stripped of any substantive meaning" (2004, p. xviii). We are reminded by Henry Giroux and Susan Giroux of the need to balance this reality by advocating a "rationale for the important and necessary use of the democratic imperative to expand individual and collective capacities to self-govern" (2004, p. 38).

Of course, one of our pressing concerns is to improve teacher education programs. This is a very active part of our work. Once again Henry Giroux is helpful. For Giroux, it seems crucial that we encourage self-reflection, learning from others, and refiguring forms of cultural practice. We have to consider how knowledge can be analyzed as opposed to giving it blind deference. In fact much of Giroux's writings center on the links of history, power, knowledge, culture, and power. For Giroux, the struggle does not stop there, but it has to be extended to rejecting the notion that the primary purpose of education is economic efficiency. Universities and schools have to be more than company stores. In fact, the very term educational reform has been denuded to mean prioritizing of curricula, lengthening of school year, teacher accountability, standardized outcomes and testing. The intrusion of the business mind-set is alarming to the point where the very foundational logic of schooling is blatantly expressed in business terms. There seems to be no attempt to question the social, cultural, or historical place of such planned reforms. Teacher education is often part of this reform muddle.

In this text we have articulated Henry Giroux's work in a particular way. Our focus is on Giroux's writings, and we attempt to locate his work in the context of our own critical pedagogy. As much as possible we are letting Giroux speak for himself under categories that we have selected to suit our purpose. We ask how we can integrate Giroux's writings in our teaching and make it effective for our teaching. We do not teach fullyfledged courses on Giroux, but his work is often the through-line for our teaching, research, and drama. In addition to that we have put great emphasis on the lived experience of our students and fellow cultural workers. We have observed, over our many years of high school and university teaching that students are struggling in many ways. They often pay a great price for their formal education. Increasingly they are under heavy debt and often hold down part-time jobs to attend university. We have noticed also that a number of students have children and are sometimes single parents. They deserve our respect. We cannot afford to treat them as if the particular course content is the only thing that matters. It is for this reason that we allow such space for students' voices. We are also concerned with the assessment of our work. Often this assessment involves students' self-evaluation, and an articulation of learning, as well as our evaluations of students' work. Student articulation of their work is evident in the *Teaching Giroux* section of the book. Like other institutions of higher learning we are governed by the mandates of our university when it comes to the mechanics of grade submission.

One of the major lessons we have learned, in interpreting and mapping Giroux's work, is to more fully realize how educational concepts evolve. One part of such a process is that existing conceptual foundations are examined, sifted, manipulated, and reconstructed in order to form new layers of understanding. These layers are then applied to everyday thought and practice and the process goes on. We realize that various scholars stand on each other's shoulders to build frameworks of language and concept. This is very evident in the acknowledgments in Giroux's books. It becomes evident that time is needed for such building. Giroux, in his earliest work, realized the complexity of education. This realization had serious implications for the development of his later work. These implications would lead him to write not only about school classrooms, but other cultural sites such as radio and film. He knew that what came in through the classroom door was far beyond text. In fact, he has done much to extend, by implication, the notion of what we mean by text. Text is much more than what is read.

As Giroux's work deepened, he would be increasingly brought back to the questions surrounding the construction of consciousness as well as the production of subjectivity. In other words, Giroux asks, how do we get to be the people we are? Such questions make any examination of the transmission of curriculum seem facile. Giroux is digging deep now. He no longer is willing to ask the easy questions. Part of his emerging answer is that power can be seen "as a concrete set of practices that produces social forms through which distinct experiences and subjectivities are shaped" (1997a, p. xi).

Giroux has proven himself to be the explorer as opposed to the mere navigator. While he might fix his gaze on a given compass point he is ever watchful for emerging stars that might guide his explorations. While some have accused him of dabbling in intellectual forms, in fact, he was always searching. If knowledge and understanding are not fixed, then such searching is essential. Otherwise we end up where we are; knowing what we know.

In teasing out a critical pedagogy, Giroux never allowed himself to be trapped into prescription. While this is often frustrating to undergraduate education students, and even classroom teachers, it is essential for development. For once you draw the lines around critical pedagogy you have lost it. Once you surround it with algorithm the search is over. The context is of paramount value here. As indicated above, Giroux never ceases to remind himself, and us, of the complexity of pedagogy. For Giroux is concerned with the making of meaning. This is a powerful phrase: the making of meaning. How do we make meaning? If this question could serve as a signpost to us each day, as we go about teaching and learning, we might be more critical.

The editors of *The Pedagogy and the Politics of Hope* tell us "without an understanding of how power is viewed by men, women, and children in specific settings, our understanding of social change remains crude, clumsy, and prone to essentialist simplification" (Giroux, 1997a, p. xiii). Giroux has been writing and teaching in a time of great educational upheaval. This upheaval is often camouflaged in seemly quiet evolution or subtle changes, but often with drastic consequences. It is our plan to examine some of these changes and consequences, as we do research on Henry A. Giroux's writings.

Reading Giroux

Chapter One

Reading the Immediate

This book is an attempt to excavate many of the primary concepts and topics found in Henry Giroux's work. These concepts then serve as a Giroux reader and as a basis for much of the educational and cultural work we do. It is certainly not meant to be exhaustive or to comment fully on the topics and concepts chosen from his wide-ranging writings. At worst it is a selection, presentation, and commentary. At best it is a textual context for his work, along with some hints at the power and influence that Henry Giroux has brought to educational, as well as cultural and social thought.

This book is built on Giroux's work, which we have collected and collated, and it covers the period from 1979 to 2005. Over this time, Giroux's thinking and writing show a remarkable evolution. It is significant to note that in many ways, he has reinvented pedagogy and now gives it a cultural and social power beyond his vision of two decades ago. With Giroux this is not surprising, for here is a person driven to understand and willing to articulate. In the final analysis Giroux keeps his eye on the prize, which is a wonderful mix of hope, possibility, and transformation. The following section of the book is the material for *Reading Giroux*. This section of the book lays the foundation for our work in education and culture that will be shared in *Teaching Giroux*.

Education

Building on the work of Cornelius Castoriadis and Raymond Williams, Giroux argues that, "Education, in the broadest sense, is a principal feature of politics because it provides the capacities, knowledge, skills, and social relations through which individuals recognize themselves as social and political agents" (Giroux, 2004, p. 115). Giroux believes that it is crucial to make a distinction between education and schooling and that makes us better able to problematize the taken-for-granted aspects of education and schooling. In much of the literature we share with each other and our students, education and schooling are often treated as interchangeable terms. This often leads to misunderstandings, inappropriate comments, and indefensible claims. However, when we see a distinction between education and schooling, we are more likely to be cautious in our comments and claims.

Giroux and Aronowitz in the influential book *Education Still Under Siege* encourage educators to ask, what is "the nature of education and what it means as a process of social and, hence, self-formation" (1993, p. 126). According to Giroux and Aronowitz, this means that educators need to involve themselves with social movements and groups that work in oppositional public spheres outside of schools, around broader educational issues. Giroux and Aronowitz use the term schooling to mean that which takes place within institutions that are directly or indirectly related to the state through funding or regulation. Education, on the other hand, is much more broadly defined, and is not limited to established institutions but can take place at many other sites. It is important to Giroux and Aronowitz that we begin to destroy the myth that education and schooling are the same thing and that "expertise and academic credentials are distinguishing marks of the intellectual; and, equally important, such educational work could also promote critical analyses of schooling itself and its relations to other institutions included in the state public sphere"(p. 129).

In an ideal fashion, at least from a critical perspective, Giroux and Aronowitz view education as representing "a collectively produced set of experiences organized around issues and concerns that allow for a critical understanding of everyday oppression as well as the dynamics involved in constructing alternative political cultures" (1993, p. 127). Ideally, such forms of learning and action would be directed toward the elimination of class, social, and gender oppression. Such intellectual development and growth, with its focus on the political, functions "to create organic intellectuals and to develop a notion of active citizenry based on self-dedication of a group of learning and social interaction that have a fundamental connection to the idea of human emancipation" (p. 127). Of course there is a real connection between education and schooling. Educators are very aware of what students bring to school with them. In other words, our students walk into school and university classes with more than we gave them the day before.

Giroux believes that there are authentic opportunities, in varied public spheres, to help develop collective power and in turn such power can be used in the development of alternative cultures. The alternative cultures, then, can get lived out in new forms of social relations and practices. We usually do not talk about education in this way. However, when we peel back the what-are-we-doing-today layers of education, we are really talking about producing meaning and cultures. Education, in the way we are talking about it here, becomes a vehicle for social mobility for those who are "privileged to have the resources and power to make their choices matter—and a form of social constraint for those who lack such resources and for whom choice and accountability reflect a legacy of broken promises and bad faith" (Giroux, 2003, pp. 80, 81).

In the introduction for *Critical Pedagogy, the State, and Cultural Struggle*, Giroux and McLaren spell out their view of public education in North America. They claim that the debate is fundamentally about the relevance of democracy, social criticism, and the meaning of our future lives. Giroux and McLaren believe that we have "failed to recognize the general relevance of education as a public service and the importance of deliberately translating educational theory into a community related discourse capable of reaching into and animating public culture and life" (1989, p. xiii). In the realm of education, Giroux and McLaren believe that students will need advanced levels of economic literacy in order to work in the marketplace. They go on to say that it is also necessary to transform that marketplace.

Giroux and McLaren are blunt in their claim that conservatives wish to rewrite the past from the perspective of the privileged and the powerful. We can readily see this in so many of the writings that represent, and are often funded by, the conservative wing in our democracy. These writings often disdain the democratic possibilities of pluralism, as well as the forms of pedagogy that critically engage issues central to developing an informed democratic public. Giroux and McLaren go on to state that there is little talk about the ethical and political demands of democratic culture and public responsibility. They believe we need to create a language of possibility. They further believe that such a language, coupled with a proactive political imagination, will resuscitate the goals of self-determination and social transformation. This is a hope far beyond propping up the status quo. The debate over education must not be about profit and elitism but about a wider struggle for democracy.

In an earlier writing, Giroux drew on a classical definition of citizenship education to claim that "a model of rationality can be recognized that is explicitly political, normative, and visionary. Within this model, education was seen as intrinsically political, designed to educate the citizen for intelligent and active participation in the civic community" (Giroux & Purpel, 1983, p. 321). In a more recent writing, *Channel Surfing* (1997b), Giroux strongly asserts that in today's world, citizenship has been replaced by an agenda that puts focus on creating consuming subjects. He goes on to state that we now operate with a very restricted notion of citizenship. In fact, this restricted notion is closely linked with a narrow definition of education where great emphasis is placed on creating a type of hyper-individualism, which has very little to do with any collective good.

In a most telling statement, Giroux says that educators need to allow students to voice their concerns. He goes on to claim that it is also crucial that we provide "the conditions-institutional, economic, spiritual, and cultural-that will allow them to reconceptualize themselves as citizens and develop a sense of what it means to fight for important social and political issues that affect their lives, bodies, and society" (1997b, p. 31). Giroux alerts us to the fact that the literacies of the postmodern age are electronic, aural, and image based, and that it is essential for us as educators to accept the reality of popular culture. It follows that we learn to incorporate into our educational understanding those aspects of popular culture that will help establish a broader vision of public life. It is also crucial that such aspects of popular culture be appropriated in a meaningful fashion. This claim will frame part of our discussion on schooling and culture.

Schooling

Giroux views schools as a resource for the larger community and as strategic sites for addressing social problems. In schools and universities students can be helped to exercise their rights and responsibilities as critical citizens. Schools and universities are much more than information mills. In our understanding of education, schooling, and pedagogy it is essential "to analyze how human experiences are produced, contested, and legitimated within the dynamics of everyday classroom life" (1997b, p. 141). Schools need to be seen as places where the dominant culture attempts to produce knowledge and subjectivities consistent with its own interest. Schools are historical and cultural institutions that are locked to some ideological and political interests. Of course, there are always individuals and groups within a community that will question the practiced ideological and policed interests. Giroux stresses that schools should not be seen merely as mirror images of the dominant society. Yet there is real tension between what is and what could be. Giroux argues that schools are agencies of moral and political regulation, and that out of such knowledge, meaning and values are produced.

The familiar refrain we hear is that schools do not serve the public interest. Giroux is quick to point out that many conservatives believe "schools have strayed too far from the logic of capital, and because of this, are now held responsible for the economic recession of the 1970s, for the loss of foreign markets to international competitors, and for the shortage of trained workers for an increasingly complex technological economy" (2005b, p. 113). Giroux and Aronowitz argue for a public philosophy that takes as "its starting point not the particularities of individual interests or forms of achievement, but the relationship of schools to the demands of active forms of community life" (1993, p. 218). The aim here is to produce forms of knowledge, pedagogy, evaluation, and research that promote critical literacy and civic courage. For Giroux and Aronowitz, schools need to be transformed into sites of learning, social interaction, and human emancipation. We believe this can be done while addressing the information and skill needs of our students, so that they can construct the next generation in democratic comfort.

As far as Giroux and Aronowitz are concerned, the elements of human agency and resistance need to be stressed. It simply is not enough to view schools as social and cultural reproductive sites. There must be an element of hope. A hope that will both challenge and change the more repressive features of schooling. In fact Giroux, in particular, has done much to develop the notion of resistance as it applies to schooling. This claim does not stop Giroux from realizing that resistance theories need to link human agency to structures and institutions. Human agency operates, in a dialogical fashion, within structures and institutions.

In relation to school and state, Giroux and Aronowitz are concerned with how the state exercises "control over schools in terms of its economic, ideological, and repressive functions? How does the school function not only to further the interests of the state and the dominant classes but also to contradict and resist the logic of capital?" (1993, p. 87). It seems to us that these are two salient questions that are able to cross the boundaries of place and time. There is little doubt that the state intervenes in schools in ways that influence the curriculum and socialization. The state has a tremendous apparatus at its disposal. The state, through its departments of education, has the means to promulgate its ideology and content, and to propose educational practices. In plain language, the state has the means to package pedagogical material and put it on teachers' desks. The logic of the process then dictates that teachers and school administrators spend their energy on adapting and implementing the new regulations and curricula.

As far as Giroux and Aronowitz are concerned, schools cannot be treated as black boxes that are the objects of domination and hegemonic control. These theorists believe that "there has been an overemphasis on how structural determinants promote economic and cultural inequality, and an under emphasis on how agency accommodates, mediates, and resists the logic of capital and its dominating social practices" (1993, p. 91). Giroux and Aronowitz believe that schools can be better understood by using notions from political science and sociology. For them, the theoretical terrains of functionalism and mainstream educational psychology simply do not explain why schools work as they do. "The notion of resistance points to the need to understand more thoroughly the complex ways in which people mediate and respond to the connection between their own experiences and structures of domination and constraint" (p. 99).

For Giroux and Aronowitz, the pedagogical value of resistance lies in the connection that it makes between structure and human agency. Schools are instructional sites, but they are also sites of struggle and contestation. Without the possibility of struggle and contestation, there can be no hope! It is our belief that much of the pedagogical struggle and contestation we read and teach about can be done in quiet ways. Transformative leaders and self-liberated teachers can change schools over time. As educators we can give ourselves the power to shift the given curriculum beyond transmission by using it as a base to interrogate local circumstances. This power can be used to nudge students on to critical thought and action.

Schools can be seen as places where teachers and students give meaning to their lives through the complex historical, cultural, and political forms they embody and produce. It follows that as educators we help our students and the teachers we work with uncover their complex histories, interests, and experiences. This must be done to counter what Giroux has called "a spurious appeal to objectivity, science, truth, universality, and the suppression of difference" (1989, p. 147).

Giroux and Roger Simon claim in *Popular Culture and Critical Pedagogy* (1989), that educational reform has been linked to the imperatives of big business. Schools, following on this perspective, can be seen as training grounds for different sectors of the work force. In addition to this, schools can be seen as providing the knowledge and occupational skills that are necessary for expanding both domestic production and foreign investment. Giroux and Simon go on to say that this particular view links schooling to the demands of a technocratic and specialized literacy that may have little to do with self-fulfillment or the common good. The many appeals to a narrowly defined Western cultural tradition that longs for a business elite and privileges the cultural capital of the ruling class groups. This conservative view cuts right across the many claims made for a critical pedagogy that affirms students from diverse social and cultural backgrounds.

Giroux believes that the traditional language about schooling is anchored in a rather mechanical and limited worldview. He says that it is a worldview borrowed primarily from "the discourse of behavioristic learning psychology, which focuses on the best way to learn a given body of knowledge, and from the logic of scientific management, as reflected in the back-to-basics movement, competency testing, and systems management schemes" (1988a, p. 2). He claims that this view of schooling is most crippling in that it limits a serious examination of ideology and language. Giroux sees the need to analyze traditional views of schooling, while offering new possibilities for both thinking about and experiencing schooling.

There is little doubt that schooling is being battered by both conservative and neoliberal critics. Schooling, because of its central and universal place in our society, is a natural target for special interest and ideological groups. This might even be healthy, especially if we can learn to see schooling in some of its complexity. We need to accept schooling as that place where more than our specific agendas are served. To begin this process it is essential to take a realistic look at schooling in North America. Giroux writes that there is a serious bid by the forces of the new right, "to replace the practice of substantive democracy with a democracy of images. At the same time, the discourse of responsible citizenship is subordinated to the marketplace imperatives of choice, consumption, and standardization" (1993a, p. 36). This approach, across North America, gets lived out overtly through drastic budget cuts, structural changes, and the most recent emphasis on standardization. On more subtle and hidden levels curriculum is being prioritized, certain forms of knowledge are being privileged, and differences are being muted. This trend is only intensified. Giroux does not allow us to ignore what he sees as the glaring disparities of class and racial inequality. Giroux sees these disparities as embedded in the very structure of schooling. Such disparities are sometimes subtle, but too often they are blatantly laid out for all to see. However, schools serve such powerful interests in our society that it is often convenient to ignore these disparities and hope they will go away. And if they do not go away, we can always blame the disparate students. Giroux warns us that we cannot ignore this reality. "Educational reform warrants more than appeals to glitzy technology and the commercialization of curricula; it needs a public discourse that makes an ethical, financial, and political investment in creating schools that educate all students to govern rather than be governed" (1994, p. 57).

Over time Giroux has been interested in developing a critical theory of schooling. First of all, he saw the need to protest against the ideological and social practices that further the mechanisms of power and domination in everyday life. Giroux believed that such a protest should move beyond "moral outrage and providing a critical account of how, within the immediate and wider dimensions of everyday life, individuals are constituted as human agents within different moral and ethical discourses and experiences" (2005b, p. 39). For Giroux a second important element of developing a critical theory of schooling had to do with developing a vision of the future. This vision, he believed, needs to be rooted in the construction of sensibilities and social relations that lead to improving human life within the framework of community.

Giroux always claimed that schools must be seen in their historical and relational contexts. For him "schooling is about the regulation of time, space, textuality, experience, knowledge, and power amid conflicting interests and histories." (1988c, p. 159). That is why it is so important for educators to understand what Giroux referred to as an ideological and political crisis surrounding the purposes of public schooling. In many ways that agenda has changed little since Giroux published the first edition of this book. Given that agenda, it is no surprise that when it was published in Great Britain, the book was given the title *Schooling for Democracy*.

One of the fundamental shifts for Giroux, over time, was to widen his critical lens from schooling as a reformative site. He came to realize that the struggle over education couldn't be limited to schools alone. He admits that while arguing that schools of education and public schooling were capable of becoming agencies of larger social reform, he "vastly underestimated both the structural and ideological constraints under which teachers labor as well as the hold that the prevailing conservatism has in shaping the curriculum and vision of most schools of education in the United States" (1993b, p. 1). It should also be noted that during this time his view of schooling was being greatly influenced by the advent of feminist theory, poststructuralism, postmodernism, cultural studies, and literary theory. For Giroux one of the fundamental mistakes being made by modern educators is a refusal to link public schooling to critical democracy. "At stake here is the refusal to grant public schooling a significant role in the ongoing process of educating people to be active and critical citizens capable of fighting for and reconstructing democratic public life" (2005a, p. 137). Giroux fully realized that we couldn't talk about schooling and ignore the political, economic, and social realities that shape schools.

Students

Henry Giroux is very concerned about youth. For him we are not just talking about a disenfranchised group in society, but he is worried about the implications for democracy itself. In *Public Time and Educated Hope* (2003c) he reminds us that we have always seen youth as embodying our hopes, dreams, and futures. Now, as we critically analyze that claim, we see more and more that in fact the voices, needs, and expectations of youth are absent from the discourse that surrounds them. They have truly become "the other." We say of our students at high school graduations and university convocations that "they are our future," yet we direct, organize, and manage them. If we do "take them into consideration," it is often only as part of our own professional or institutional mandate. We often see this as we reformulate or develop public school or university curriculum. Students' voices are often quite literally dismissed.

It is in such a climate that Henry Giroux sees an "impoverished sense of politics and public life, [where] the public school is gradually being transformed into a training ground for 'the corporate workforce'"(2003b, p. 5). We need to be wary when we are told that we are graduating "good people;" it often means we are graduating useful people. In Giroux's terms we need to retain at least part of secondary education as "an important site for investing public life with substance and vibrancy" (p. 7). In time Henry Giroux came to the conclusion that students must be offered the opportunity to engage the multiple references that "constitute different cultural codes, experiences, and languages. This means educating students to both read those codes historically and critically while simultaneously learning the limits of such codes, including the ones they use to construct their own narratives and histories" (2005a, p. 108). This challenge goes far beyond the transmission of the informational content that fills many classroom days. We are not suggesting that such content is not significant, but as Giroux would argue, it is simply not enough in itself. The transmission of information, whether it is history, science, or civic duty and then gathering it back in the form of tests and essays, will not prepare students for democracy.

Students need to begin by respecting their own cultures. This means that their cultures need to be affirmed if they are to be the building blocks of learning. If we can begin by sharing our students' beliefs, values, and experiences we can then encourage them to bring the wider world into their frames of reference. Then they can cross borders. We sometimes act as if we can inject knowledge, critical thinking, and transformative consciousness into students. We are better educators if we encourage them to examine the social, cultural, economic, and political forces that impinge on their lives.

Giroux contends that it is a poor pedagogy where a "student's voice is reduced to the immediacy of its performance, existing as something to be measured, administered, registered, and controlled" (1997b, p. 124). As experienced teachers, we realize that it is very difficult to teach if we are preoccupied with classroom management. Yet classrooms have to be "managed" as a basic requirement for teaching and learning. We have to somehow draw students into the endeavor of pedagogy. This means, in part, sharing the learning with them. As long as we insist on operating as "the ones who know," we are doomed to a lonely place standing in front of our students. If we are to go beyond the borders of our own knowing, then we must become learners. Students appreciate the fact that we are willing to learn with them. This does not mean that we play the same role as the students do in the learning process. Teachers and students have different responsibilities within the pedagogy.

In his earlier writings, Giroux put forward a salient point by stating that "Students bring different histories to school; these histories are embedded in class, gender, and race interests that share their needs and behavior, often in ways they don't understand or that work against their own interests" (1983, p. 149). It is crucial for all students to be able to critically examine their own values, beliefs, and experiences in the face of other values, beliefs, and experiences. It is not easy for students to temper their own values and beliefs because they are embedded in culture. Such values and beliefs, and the experiences that grow out of them, are often treated as given and fixed. We believe, following Giroux's lead, that students can be gently teased out of this fixed state into believing that there is the need and the possibility of change. Giroux cuts to the quick when he states "students as well as teachers are intellectuals and need to see themselves as informed political agents" (1991, p. 118). Part two of this book indicates, in some fashion, how we encourage students to realize their own agency.

Students need "to draw upon their own experiences and cultural resources and that also enables them to play a self-consciously active role as producers of knowledge within the teaching and learning process" (Giroux & McLaren, 1989, p. 148). In schools, students need to get the knowledge and skills that allow them to interrogate the texts, institutions, and social structures around them in a way that helps them produce authentic knowledge.

In *Channel Surfing*, the category of student is subsumed under the category of youth. This work helps fill Giroux's view of those young people who inter-act with, and bounce off, pedagogy and culture. Giroux writes that there must be "a recognition that the category of youth is constituted across diverse languages and cultural representations as well as racial and class based experiences" (1997b, p. 4). Once again we are reminded, "how we understand and come to know ourselves and others cannot be separated from how we are represented and imagine ourselves" (p. 14). This book takes on a heavy moral terrain when Giroux suggests that we, as educators, have a responsibility to help prepare future generations to confront the world we have created.

In holding up representations of youth found in advertisements and popular forums, Giroux wishes to see them in relation to pedagogical work. He is interested in "what knowledge, values, and pleasures such representations invite or exclude. What particular forms of identity, agency, and subjectivity are privileged, and how do they help to reinforce dominant reactions, messages, and meanings?" (1997b, p. 27). This, to us, seems like a very important agenda. After all, in our interactions with students through the pedagogy and the culture we share, it is crucial that we understand such things. Otherwise we are "talking to the wall" or contributing to "dead time." How can we have a pedagogy that affirms students' beliefs, values, and experiences and yet know nothing about their culture and its representations? "Educationally and politically, young people need to be given the opportunity to narrate themselves, to speak from the actual places where their experiences and daily lives are shaped and mediated" (p. 31). Giroux reminds us that young peoples' experiences and daily lives are formed by alternative music, various subcultures, mass media, underground magazines, and many other sites. It follows that there is some pedagogical responsibility for us to know about these forums.

Teachers

According to Henry Giroux teachers and professors need to work with a language of possibility and develop a curriculum that draws on and affirms, the cultural resources which students bring to schools and universities. In addition, he says, that teachers and professors need to be able to critically examine the values, beliefs, and mind-sets, and agenda's we bring to class. In this way we have a more hopeful opportunity to help develop a sense of identity, community, and possibility. While admitting the constraints that teachers work under, Giroux believes that they hold great transformative potential. He realized early on in his academic life that teachers needed to critically examine the work they do. In part, this means that teachers need to "develop pedagogical theories and methods that link self-reflection and understanding with a commitment to change the nature of the larger society" (1981, p. 58). In many ways much of Henry Giroux's work has been dedicated to helping teachers live out their potential as an emancipatory force. Part of his suggestion is that teachers stop seeing themselves as "impartial facilitators who operate in a value-free and ideologically uncontaminated classroom setting" (p. 80). The work of teachers is not neutral.

In particular Giroux has been interested in how teachers interact with the knowledge they use. Part of our task, as educators, is to help "strip away the unexamined reality that hides behind the objectivism and fetishism of 'facts' in positive pedagogy" (1997a, p. 24). When we treat knowledge as social constructs, then we will be free to deal with such knowledge as less than privileged and less than sacred. In many instances, teachers are learning to examine the work they do in ways that transform educational sites. However, in the face of this promise, there are the obstacles of centrally developed curriculum, teaching to standards, and job insecurity.

Giroux has contributed greatly to this struggle with the development of the concept of teacher as transformative intellectual. Part of Giroux's agenda is to see teaching as a form of cultural politics that needs to be understood as a set of practices that produces social forms through which different types of knowledge, sets of experience, and subjectivities are constructed. Giroux believes that "transformative intellectuals need to understand how subjectivities are produced and regulated through historically produced social forms and how these forms carry and embody particular interests" (1988a, p. xxxv). This is what we describe in the second part of the book. On top of realizing how subjectivities are produced and regulated, Giroux stresses that we need to investigate how power works its way through certain forms of knowledge that privilege selected truths and life views. In relation to this, Giroux encourages teachers to place teaching in the realm of cultural work. He reminds us that we work with our students in teaching and learning sites that have been developed within specific modes of "textual, verbal, and visual practices which we hope will provoke particular forms of communication, comprehension, and interest. How we fashion this engagement, within what value-based projects and with what corresponding strategies and questions, defines much of our pedagogical practice" (1994, p. 93).

The true significance of teaching can be better realized when we get some glimpse of the power we have to construct and manipulate ways of knowing, forms of knowledge, values, social practices, and belief systems. It can be questioned if any other professional has such power. In the final analysis the power of teachers is lived out more by confronting how we understand how society is shaped than by acute refinements of method, content, and resources. Giroux is quite succinct in claiming that we need to guard against the separation of "conception from execution; the standardization of school knowledge in the interest of managing and controlling it; and the devaluation of critical, intellectual work on the part of teachers and students for the primacy of practical considerations" (1988a, p. 123). Giroux is also quite astute in calling for teachers to be transformative intellectuals because these terms are filled with salient messages. By this he means that teachers understand the nature of their own self-formation; see the importance of education as a public discourse; and have a sense of mission in providing students what they need to become critical citizens.

Too often teaching is thought of in technical terms. In fact, much of the rhetoric on educational reform is based on the simplistic logic of improved teacher training and improved methodologies. Teaching is a process that demands the integration of thinking and practice. This view is quite in keeping with the work done by Schon (1983, 1987) and others in relation to the reflective practitioner. Much of the content offered teachers is prepackaged in a way that separates curriculum development and implementation. Teachers are treated as if their sole purpose is to deliver the curriculum conceived, planned, and designed by some central agency.

We believe that many teachers are equipped by intelligence and education to be transformative intellectuals but are burdened by the demand that they serve certain economic, social, and historical roles. Teachers need to see the work they do as political work. For it is certainly that. If we are to follow on Giroux's thinking we need to help each other develop a discourse that unites the language of critique with the language of possibility. If we are to do this, we have to speak out against economic, political, and social injustices both within and outside of schools. In addition to this, we must work to create the conditions that give students the opportunity to become active citizens. Once again we can readily see that Giroux's writings about teachers must be viewed in the nexus of other significant conceptual areas. The role of teachers cannot be understood without reference to the place of schooling, the power of ideology, and the needs of democracy, as well as the other spheres that help explain how personal identity and social reality get constructed.

Giroux and Aronowitz, writing in *Education Still Under Siege*, claim that teachers need to be public and transformative intellectuals: "That is, intellectuals who are part of a specific class, group, or movement and who serve to give it coherence and an awareness of its own function in the economic, social, and political fields" (1994, p. 155). In this scenario, teachers need to be aware that they are dancing between the dominant culture and everyday life and that their role is political. Teachers, as transformative intellectuals, not only need to check the social terrain where they work, but they also need to examine their own histories. They further need to help break down the division between intellectual and manual labour. This division lies at the separation between teacher thinking and teacher doing; at the disjuncture between curriculum development and curriculum implementation; and at the normative split between theory and practice. Reflection on these issues is crucial for all of us, no matter where we work. This certainly is not a discourse about the other.

In the final analysis, teachers need to operate with the language and perspective of hope. This is very much at odds with the view that schools are merely zones of management. Part of the process of operating with a language and perspective of hope is locked to a practice of teachers producing and adapting curricula materials suited to the cultural and social contexts in which they teach. Teachers are continually expected to deliver a curricula developed by someone else, for someone else's students.

Giroux and Aronowitz claim that viewing teachers as intellectuals is locked to the rather general notion that all human activity involves some form of thinking. "We dignify the human capacity for integrating thinking and practice, and in doing so we highlight the care of what it means to view teachers as reflective practitioners" (1994, p. 40). Giroux and Aronowitz stress that with this view of teacher as intellectual comes a matching responsibility. The role of intellectual is much more than a mantel placed on teachers by some academic or education functionary. It is in fact a responsibility; for some, a burden. The role of intellectual for teachers means that they must "take responsible roles in shaping the purposes and conditions of schooling." They go on to stress that such a task "is impossible within a division of labor where teachers have little influence over the ideological and economic conditions of work" (p. 40). Of course this is not easy. The grounding for such work rests, in part, with the realization of the need and significance of the pedagogical and cultural work. In plain language, where will we be if the work is not done? We see little choice but to do such work. Some of our efforts are presented in this book and elsewhere.

Language

Giroux reminds us that one of the most important elements at work in the construction of experience and subjectivity is language. Because language is intimately related to power, it "functions to both position and constitute the way that teachers and students define, mediate, and understand their relations to each other, school knowledge, the institutions of schooling, and the larger society" (Giroux & McLaren, 1989, p. 143). As far as Giroux is concerned, the notion that meaning is constituted in language is a crucial insight. He couples this insight with the belief that individuals construct meaning out of their own histories and boundaries. Therefore, in a real sense, individuals construct meaning out of language and practice. That is why it is so crucial for teachers to work with, and build on, the knowledge experiences that students have. Such work is not merely a pedagogical trick to have students learn what teachers want them to learn. Students' previous knowledge and experience is the foundation of new learning. Giroux believes that it is essential to provide a language of possibility. By this he means a language that helps us pedagogically and politically "to provide the conditions for rethinking a new type of social agent, one that could individually and collectively imagine a global society that combines freedom and social justice modeled after the imperatives of a radical and inclusive democracy" (2003a, p. 58).

As in other theoretical spheres, Giroux has salient thoughts on the importance and place of language in our society. "The notion of language is evaluated according to whether it is simple or complex, clear or vague, concrete or abstract. However, this analysis falls prey to a theoretical error; it reduces language to a technical issue, i.e., the issue of clarity" (1988a, p. 2). But the real meaning of educational language has to be understood as the product of a specific theoretical framework, via the assumptions that govern it, and finally, through the social, political, and ideological relations to which it points and which it legitimates. Giroux believes that when we place emphasis on the issue of clarity in working with language, we often downplay questions about values and interests.

While the traditional conventions of communication call for speaking and writing in a language that is clear and unambiguous, Giroux is adamant in claiming that new ideas often require new terms. It follows that new terms follow on new ideas. We realize that calling particular language forms ambiguous, obtuse, or jargon is often an attack on the content or the author. Attacking the language is often enough to disallow the argument. As Giroux warns, we have to be careful that the call for clarity does not suppress difference. He argues for "a theory of language that not only recognizes the importance of complexity and difference but also provides the conditions for educators to cross borders, where disparate linguistic, theoretical, and political realities meet" (1993a, p. 157).

Giroux claims that language should be studied not only as a technical and expressive device, but also as an active agent in the production of various texts and institutional powers. In other words, language needs to be seen as a formative as well as an expressive force. Giroux sees the debate over language to be a crucial one, and he reasons that educators need to deal with the issue of language as a matter of politics. This is where a connection between language and power needs to be made. "Language is situated in an ongoing struggle over issues of inclusion and exclusion, meaning and interpretation, and such issues are inextricably related to questions of 'power, history, and self identity' " (1993a, p. 161). Giroux believes language is inseparable from the lived experience of people. In the same text, he goes on to claim that language is strongly connected to the struggle among different groups over "what will count as meaningful and whose cultural capital will prevail in legitimating particular ways of life" (p. 116). This claim is significant for teachers and students, who in their daily dealings with each other and with the curriculum content, struggle, even in quiet ways, for acceptance and dominance. For example, teachers might genuinely believe that the language they use is neutral; that it does not affirm one student over another; and that it does not privilege one form of knowledge over another. As teachers, we want to believe that our language is inclusive and embracing. This is not always true. Beyond the techniques of pitch, tone, and diction our language has the power to hurt, heal, and help.

One of the foundational claims made by Giroux is that school language is defined in technical terms or communicative value. By seeing language in these ways it is "abstracted from its political and ideological usage" (1997a, p. 131). Language, along with all its uses, needs to help students affirm, validate, and critically engage their own experiences and cultures. Educators, if we see ourselves as public intellectuals can "teach students what might be called a language of social criticism and responsibility; a language that refuses to treat knowledge as something to be consumed passively, taken up merely to be tested, or legitimated outside of an engaged normative discourse" (Giroux, 2000, p. 35). Giroux's thinking about language is heavily indebted to the work of Mikhail Bakhtin and Paulo Freire. Giroux sees Bakhtin's work as important in that he, Bakhtin, "views language use as an eminently social and political act linked to the ways individuals define meaning and author their relations to the world through an ongoing dialogue with others" (1997a, p. 132). Freire, according to Giroux, "offers the possibility for organizing pedagogical experiences within social forms and practices that 'speak' to developing more critical and dialogical modes of learning and struggle" (132). Giroux's work, along with Bakhtin's and Freire's, points to a use of language that is grounded in the context of everyday life and that asks how human experiences are produced, contested, and legitimated within classrooms.

In a powerful chapter called "Rethinking the Boundaries of Educational Discourse," Giroux probes the various facets of language as it applies to our daily work as educators. He is most helpful when he encourages teachers, as part of their use of a language of possibility, to "create knowledge/power relations in which multiple narratives and social practices are constructed around a politics and pedagogy of difference that offers students the opportunity to read the world differently, resist the abuse of power and privilege, and envision alternative democratic communities" (1997a, p. 220). In practical terms Giroux would have us, as he does himself, allow students to find their own voices through their culturally produced language, in ways that express what they know, what they are experiencing, and what they are learning. This is the stuff of critical pedagogy.

Voice

Part of our overt agenda in this book has been to explore, in an active way, the concept and practice of voice. In this part of the book we allow, as much as possible, Henry Giroux's voice to be heard. In part two we allow the voices of our students, colleagues, and fellow cultural workers to be heard. We now more fully realize that voice is not something that we, as educators, can give to students. It is something to be engaged and critically understood. Voice is not unproblematic, yet it is central to any sense of agency. As part of a process of agency, we encourage students to engage Giroux's writings at four sites: teacher internship, classroom teaching, research, and various sites for cultural productions. The challenge is more than encouraging students to read Giroux's writings. For us the more crucial and desired aspect of this agenda is to empower students through the pedagogical processes and sites we use. This means we have to open up these sites to students and teachers. If our students can produce "local theories" about what they do at these sites, they might empower themselves and then speak with more confidence about such crucial issues as substantive democracy, citizenship, race, youth, media, and other concerns. As we will spell out in the *Teaching Giroux* part of this book, we try to create sites in which students can practice articulating their voices in order to empower themselves. In this process we try to critically understand the context and complexity of various voices. In writing this book we are claiming that integrating Giroux's writings into pedagogical practices gives us a place to engage the voices of students, as well as our own.

It is helpful for us to use the concept of voice as a pedagogical category. This exercise allows us to ask what students bring to school and university as well as to realize the knowledge and culture students and teachers can produce between them. Following on Giroux, we believe that knowledge, and the production of knowledge can be made more relevant to the world of the students. It is helpful for professors and teachers to realize that they can collaborate with their students to transform, where necessary, aspects of lived experiences. This cannot be done in a vacuum. We see transformation working in an analogous fashion to hegemony. Transformation, which should be allowed to seep through our institutions and relationships, usually comes in small doses and usually happens over time. Transformation often happens through cultural production. We will examine this possibility in a section called Cultural Production, in the last part of this text.

As educators, we sometimes confuse loud for voice. Authentic student voices have little to do with decibels. For many reasons we speak out of our lived experience. Therefore, if we are not free to speak out of our experiences, we might not have any voice. If individual experience is negated, is it possible that the individual is negated? Silenced? We believe that Giroux is encouraging us to use our various pedagogical projects to help students speak around these silences (1993b). With careful pedagogies we can help give voice to student experiences, and therefore to students. One of the concepts that we are interested in is the one of student authorship. Giroux addresses this possibility in *Pedagogy and the Politics of Hope* (1997a), when he incorporates student authorship into his classroom teaching. He is very conscious not to distance students from their histories and lived experiences. His answer was to use what he called, "border writing" (p. 172). He linked the use of writing assignments to encouraging students to theorize their own experiences. This invitation is taken up in the *Teaching Giroux* part of the text. We believe that the stories and experiences of students can serve as the material for student authorship, and therefore voice.

Once students realize that authors usually write out of their own culture they can see that such cultural production can be theirs. Here students can find their voice. Once students come to the realization that their authorship is liberating, they can build on that freedom. Students can use their authorship to "reconstitute their relationship within the wider society" (Giroux, 1988c, p. 153). Part of the struggle for voice, in pedagogy, is to help develop a language that can serve as a means to empower students to socially transform their lives. In this context, we are not limiting voice to speaking. Voice comes in many forms. For example, if students can develop a text for fiction, they might be able to produce a voice that speaks to their own reality. This transformation is accomplished over time by building layers of confidence and self-critique. In the safe space of fictional language, spoken or written, students can find their voices. As Giroux would caution us, we need to spend less time on the technical skills of voicing and more time on "a form of cultural production that more closely articulated the relationship between my political project as a progressive teacher and the underlying principles and practices that informed the organization and character of my class" (p. 171).

Giroux also reminds us that as teachers we need to examine our own voices as they "actively produce, sustain, and legitimate meaning and experience in classrooms" (2005b, p. 159). Part of our pedagogical agenda, as we maneuver between transmission and transformation, is to lay out the possibility for students to probe their own reality. It follows that we have to try and build on the cultural capital of students. We need to help students realize the authentic value of their different lifestyles, ethnic origins, and belief systems. All of these differences can help make up the mosaic of a critical pedagogy. Giroux sees this mosaic as the place where knowledge, language, and power intersect. This intersection can be a site where moral, cultural, and social practices are produced. Can we expect less from our pedagogical work?

As we have claimed earlier, one of the intentions of educators working in schools and universities can be simply to allow students to explore their own voices. As Giroux has pointed out, university students can be as silent, and silenced, as any public school student. We are apt to forget that sometimes the exploring of student voice is much more important than the presentation of new material. Teachers and professors can simply give students a place to speak their authentic part. Students are able to use their experiences, their cultures, and their stories, to better understand their place in society. This in itself is a real form of power for students. This is voice power.

An agenda that authentically calls for student voices demands a classroom setting that allows for sharing and dialogue. In particular, students need to physically face each other. The physical form of the classroom speaks to the quality of the process. Schools are not like old churches, where the very structure of the place demands silence. Expecting students to tell their stories, share their heritage, and voice their dreams to the backs of fellow students' heads is patently ridiculous. It should be noted that we are quite aware of teacher concerns for classroom management. In another place we have written about the "Reflective Internship and the Phobia of Classroom Management" (Singh, Doyle, Rose, Kennedy, 1997; Singh, 2001). Another significant factor in critical pedagogy is the teacher's voice. We believe, at the risk of overstatement, that the authentic voice of the teacher and professor is the single greatest tool in developing a critical pedagogy. The teacher, or the professor, is a gatekeeper between the dominant culture of the school or university and the individual student. We need to learn to use the language of a truly critical pedagogy to free rather than to confuse. This language and these skills can also serve as gate openers. We can use students' own stories, their own voices, to foster a critical pedagogy for their students.

Reading Place

Democracy

Giroux believes, as many of us do, that these are dark days for democracy. In the powerful *Terror of Neoliberalism,* he claims "Within the discourse of neoliberalism, democracy becomes synonymous with free markets while issues of equality, social justice, and freedom are stripped of any substantive meaning and used to disparage those who suffer systemic deprivation and chronic punishment" (2004, p. xviii). Giroux understands that in dealing with the reality of democracy it is important for teachers and students to approach the problems of adult life. "Such knowledge includes not only the basic skills students need to work and live in the wider society, but also knowledge about the social forms through which humans live, become conscious, and sustain themselves" (1997a, p. 108). This includes, according to Giroux, knowledge about power, racism, sexism, and class exploitation. In relation to this quest, schools and universities need to be viewed as democratic spheres. In such spheres the skills of democracy can be practiced, debated, and analyzed.

Taking up the battle for democracy on another front, Giroux insists that universities need to operate as democratic public spheres. "Fundamental to the rise of a vibrant democratic culture is the recognition that education must be treated as a public good and not merely as a site for commercial investment or for affirming a notion of the private good based exclusively on the fulfillment of individual needs" (2001, p. 33). We believe that universities are, in many ways, the least of democratic places, because they are so burdened by tradition and canon. This thought, and the claims made around it, will be examined more closely in the probe on Giroux's understanding of higher education.

Giroux stresses that there needs to be a political and ethical foundation for a democratic life. A significant part of Giroux's agenda is to help in the process of reconstructing democratic life. A major step towards this reconstruction is to help students "with the opportunity to develop the critical capacity to challenge and transform existing social and political forms, rather than simply adapt to them" (1997a, p. 218). This means, according to Giroux, that students need to be able to locate themselves in history, find their own voices, and take democratic risks. Of course this critical capacity is needed for all of us. Giroux reminds us that democracy has much to do with "having access to the technological and cultural resources necessary to be informed, make decisions, and to exercise control over the material and ideological forces that govern peoples' lives" (1993a, p. 12). It seems that part of Giroux's worry is that the goal of democracy is losing its appeal and sense of urgency. He believes that part of the legacy we can leave our children and students is the ideal of democracy as a goal worth believing in and struggling for.

Culture

Henry Giroux and Susan Searls Giroux place great value on culture. "Culture is recognized as the social field where goods and social practices are not only produced, distributed, and consumed, both also invested with various meanings and ideologies that have widespread political effects" (Giroux & Giroux, 2004, p. 90). For them culture not only reflects larger forces in society but also constitutes them. Culture not only mediates history, but also shapes it. One of the real accomplishments of critical pedagogy has been to help give culture its place in the discourse of schooling and education. Of course this is not to claim that all who live by pedagogy are enamored of culture. Culture is a very elusive concept. It might even be said that once you define culture you have lost it. Even a cursory glance at Henry Giroux's books and journal articles would indicate the significant place that culture holds in his thinking. Giroux builds on the notion that culture is "a form of production, specifically, as the ways in which human beings make sense of their lives, feelings, beliefs, thoughts, and wider society" (1997a, p. 125). He fully realizes that culture plays its part in shaping identities, values, and histories. Giroux uses the term culture to signify the way a particular social group lives out and makes sense of its reality. This use of culture involves both practices and ideologies. Giroux fully realizes that there is a crucial link between culture and power. Given these factors, it follows that culture has to be an important ingredient in the mix of schooling and education.

What is essential in reading this aspect of Giroux's work is to appreciate that any given particular culture needs to be viewed in its context. The content of culture must be seen as being produced in a given space, place, and time. The traditional concept of culture, as Giroux articulated it in one of his earlier works, "contributed little to an understanding of how power functions in a society so far as to structure its various socio-economic classes, institutions, and social practices" (1981, p. 26). The traditional notion of culture is seen as separate from such significant concepts as class, power, and conflict. This critical stance on the place of culture has been the grounding for much of Giroux's evolving work, for in many ways, culture has been the theoretical vehicle to move our thinking about schooling and education beyond the transmission of dominant traditions, values, and content. Culture has also been the center of a conceptual web that stretches out to ensnare the factors of history, politics, and economics that need to be part of our understanding of schooling and education.

Giroux was never content to view culture in its naive sense. For him "culture is more than an expression of experiences forged within the social and economic spheres of a given society; it is the latter and more. It is a complex realm of antagonistic experiences mediated by power and struggle" (1981, p. 27). For example, the proponents of cultural studies have been concerned with "culture as something that is unfinished, incomplete, and always in process. Knowledge and beliefs are not rendered legitimate or useful by virtue of their production within specific disciplines nor to the indebtedness to what is alleged to be western culture" (Giroux & Shannon, 1997, p. 238).

It is important to remember that Giroux, even in his earlier writings, realized that culture is also the site where human beings can shape and transform their lives. This element of hope has always been present in his work. As we get a sense of how Giroux uses the concept of culture, we begin to see why he has been able to stretch the parameters of how we now view schooling and education. Writing in *Popular Culture, Schooling and Everday Life* Giroux and Simon claim that educators who do not acknowledge popular culture as a significant basis of knowledge "often devalue students by refusing to work with the knowledge that students actually have and so eliminate the possibility of developing a pedagogy that links school knowledge to the differing subject relations that help to constitute their everyday lives" (1989, p. 3). Giroux and

Simon argue that when we ignore the cultural and social forms of youth, we run the risk of silencing and negating them. If we really want to understand how student identities, cultures, and experiences provide a basis for learning, we certainly need to understand the cultural worlds of students.

As part of this discussion on culture, Giroux and Simon claim that popular culture is organized around the investments of pleasure and fun; is located in everyday life; and is a major source of knowledge for authorizing their voices and experiences. As far as Giroux and Simon are concerned, we need to ask such significant questions as: What relationship is there between classroom work and students' lives outside the class? Is it possible to incorporate aspects of students' culture into schoolwork in a fashion that goes beyond merely confirming what they already know? Can we incorporate students' culture without trivializing it?

Giroux and Aronowitz, writing in *Education Still Under Siege*, state that traditionally school culture has operated as an aspect of high culture. "The teacher's job was to transmit this culture to students in the hope that it would offset those cultural forms reproduced on the terrains of popular culture and subordinate class experience" (1993, p. 230). The culture wars waged over the last decade bear this claim out. The debate over what should constitute school culture was never more vital than it is at the present time. This debate ranges from the strident demands for a return to classical Western culture in our schools and universities to the calls for texts that reflect the varied ethnic, racial, and gender voices and images that pepper our society. Certainly there is room for Toni Morrison to sit on the same library shelf with William Shakespeare. Possibly one of the strongest symbols a teacher or instructor can use is to display those varied voices.

In the view of Giroux and McLaren, "popular culture represents not only a contradictory terrain of struggle, but also a significant pedagogical site that raises important questions about the elements that organize the basis of student subjectivity and experience" (1989, p. 238). Behind this view is a notion of culture as a public sphere where the basic principles and practices of democracy are learned amid struggle, difference, and dialogue. Giroux reminds us in *Channel Surfing*, that "popular culture is contradictory; it is also responsible for unleashing a torrent of youthful creativity in the arts, public access radio, dance, video, film, underground journals, and computer bulletin boards" (1997b, p. 33). Giroux does a wonderful job of revealing and interrogating the contradictions of popular culture in his books *Channel Surfing, Living Danger-*

ously, *Impure* *Acts,* *The* *Mouse* *That* *Roared,* and *Breaking* *into* *the* *Movies.* Of course these themes are taken up elsewhere as well. These texts are researched and written in a fashion that allows us as educators to realize, in some small way, the crucial relevance of the movie we see, the text we read, and the advertisement we hear. We know that the movies, videos, texts, and the advertisements are far beyond entertainment. In fact we cannot contain these forms as entertainment. These cultural moments invite, form, and represent us: we produce them, yet they also work to construct and reconstruct us. Much like Giroux's work helps construct and reconstruct us as educators.

Cultural Capital

In Giroux's earlier work, the concept of cultural capital was a dominant one. This work was greatly influenced by the writings of Pierre Bourdieu. While Giroux might be distancing himself from the use of the term there seems to be little doubt that the significance of the concept lies beneath much of his writings. While Giroux might have expanded his notion of the place of cultural capital, he has not pulled back from his belief that members of a given community "wage a constant battle for a portion of society's cultural capital through curriculum and pedagogy" (1981, p. 3). Of course, Giroux now appreciates the fact that people are formed not only through curriculum and pedagogy but also through the multitude of cultural sites that dot our personal landscapes. Giroux and Aronowitz, writing in *Education* *Still* *Under* *Siege,* claim that "schools play a particularly important role in legitimating certain forms of knowledge, ways of speaking, and ways of relating to the world that capitalize on the type of familiarity and skills that only certain students have received from family background and class relations" (1994, p. 76).

In a basic fashion, cultural capital can be seen as the legitimization of "certain forms of knowledge, language practices, values, modes of style, and so forth" (Giroux, 1988a, p. 5). In an earlier writing, Giroux had cautioned that we inherit from our families "sets of meanings, qualities of style, modes of thinking, and types of dispositions that are accorded a certain social value and status as a result of what the dominant class or classes label as most valued cultural capital" (1983, p. 88). While Giroux has gone on to name and interrogate other areas of influence in forming identities, personal meanings, values, and practices, the notion of cultural capital was certainly a seminal one. We continue to introduce this concept to our students.

In a more recent writing, Giroux makes use of the term cultural capital when he reminds us that "schooling often functions to affirm the Eurocentric, patriarchal histories, social identities, and cultural experiences of middle-class students while either marginalizing or erasing the voices, experiences, and cultural memories of so-called minority students" (Giroux & Shannon, 1997, p. 233). As we indicated earlier, the form in which these topics are presented in this book are certainly not meant to indicate that any topic, such as cultural capital, can be understood in isolation. In so many ways such topics can be seen as evolving moments in Henry Giroux's thinking and our knowledge.

Giroux and Aronowitz stress the need for teachers to develop forms of knowledge and classroom social practices that validate the experiences students bring with them to school. The belief is that if students can speak out of their own experiences then they can have a more active voice. Too often many of our students are silenced. Not from any malice, but because as educators and teachers we affirm types of values, backgrounds, and experiences that are often alien to them. This is where the care of our students becomes a factor. Giroux and Aronowitz believe that this care demands, "acknowledging the language forms, style of presentation, dispositions, forms of reasoning, and cultural forms that give meaning to student experiences" (1993, p. 151). This means linking the cultural capital of all students to the curriculum. These beliefs inform our discussions with students.

There is little doubt that schools legitimize the dominant cultural capital through the selection of given beliefs and skills. Those students who best accept and replicate the dominant curricula are the ones most affirmed. They are the ones most successful. Other students are marginalized because of language styles, social practices, or cultural experiences that do not mirror the dominant cultural chic. We believe this is an insidious problem in many social settings. It is a problem exacerbated by teacher education professors, administrators, teachers, and students themselves. Students can be merciless on each other. This is most evident in the formation and rituals of school cliques. These cliques are often formed around symbols of cultural capital: language, dress, and race. They most always represent exclusion, and one of the most difficult moments for teachers does center on dealing with the excluded. This reality is no less evident in university classes.

In our attempts to understand the notion of cultural capital, Giroux and Aronowitz would have us go beyond the category of domination and realize that resistance and hope are possible. They accept that Pierre Bourdieu's notion of cultural capital is significant in that it provides a theoretical model of understanding aspects of schooling and social control that had been generally ignored in education. Giroux and Aronowitz, however, would wish to put more emphasis on reflective thought and historical agency in the cause of resistance. They further want to stress that culture is both a structuring and transforming process.

Cultural Studies

There is little doubt that Henry Giroux has had tremendous effect on how we view education and schooling. This is true, in part, because he saw the need to extend the understanding of the many factors that influence education and schooling. He was aware of how technology, specifically the media of mass communication, played its part in forming identities, attitudes, and practices. For him the process of representation through popular culture became important. Now it seemed a logical step for Giroux to look to cultural studies as an umbrella space to help examine his expanding theoretical interests. The editors of *Pedagogy and the Politics of Hope* Kincheloe, McLaren and Steinberg write: "Using the interdisciplinary and transdisciplinary tools of cultural studies to translate theory into democratic practice, Giroux continues to expand the intellectual envelope in his search for new modes of academic enterprise" (Giroux, 1997a, p. xiii). They rightly claim that Giroux has provided new understandings of the pedagogical process and helped return cultural studies to its pedagogical roots. Henry Giroux and Susan Searls Giroux know that cultural studies help us understand that "culture deploys power and is shaped and organized within diverse systems of representation, production, consumption, and distribution" (2004, p. 90). As indicated in *Take back Higher Education* and elsewhere, it is clear that one of Henry Giroux's great contributions is in theorizing, "the regulatory and emancipatory relationship among culture, power, and politics as expressed through the dynamics of what we call public pedagogy" (p. 95).

Culture is one of the most significant concepts in Giroux's work. Any exegesis of this work clearly indicates that culture is a crucial lens for viewing education and schooling. Therefore it is not difficult to see how cultural studies would become such an important area of study for him. Still, he is quick to admit that it is becoming difficult to assess what is the nature of the power and practice of cultural studies. However, Giroux believes that because cultural studies emerged outside the university, and therefore outside the canon of official knowledge, it is allowed to be political and oppositional. Giroux indicates that cultural studies has become "one of the few radically innovative fields to have traveled across multiple borders and spaces, loosely uniting a diverse group of intellectuals who challenge conventional understandings of the relationship among culture, power, and politics" (Giroux & Shannon, 1997, p. 231). Douglas Kellner claims "Giroux thus uses cultural studies to transform and enrich critical pedagogy and to provide new intellectual tools and practices to transform education" (Giroux & Myrsiades, 2001, p. 142). That is exactly what he does!

Giroux refers to the work of Raymond Williams in relation to the emergence of cultural studies in Birmingham, England. Williams explained that cultural studies grew out of the work being done in adult education in the 1930s and 1940s. This, in part, is the base Giroux uses to reclaim the place of pedagogy in present cultural studies. As far as Giroux is concerned, cultural studies "represents an ensemble of diverse discourses, it is an important historical, political, and cultural formation that points to a number of issues that need to be addressed in pedagogical terms" (1997a, p. 165). Giroux acknowledges the work that cultural critics have done to create critical discourses and forms of social criticism and to make the political visible.

> Rejecting the well-policed distinctions that pit form against content, professionalism against politics, and subjective experience against objective representations, many critical educators and cultural-studies theorists have endeavored in different ways to break down the rigid boundaries and binary oppositions between teaching and politics, ethics and power, high and low culture, margins and centers, and so on. (Giroux & Shannon, 1997, p. 6)

Giroux states that cultural studies is largely defined through the way it analyzes the relationship between culture and power. In cultural studies, there is a particular emphasis on the diverse use of texts. It should also be remembered that the term text is used here in a very wide sense. "In the most general sense, cultural studies signifies a massive shift away from Eurocentric master narratives, disciplinary knowledge, high culture, scientism, and other legacies informed by the diverse heritage of modernism" (Giroux & Shannon, 1997, p. 234). Giroux believes that cultural studies is a shifting force, never allowed to fix itself in the cement of formula or tradition. It must constantly reconstruct itself to deal with new realities as they arise. It amazes Giroux that cultural studies and pedagogy are not more closely linked. He seems particularly concerned that cultural studies have not been taken up by educational reformers as well as by colleges and schools of education. Giroux writes that cultural studies is "premised on the belief that the traditional distinctions that separate and frame established academic disciplines cannot account for the great diversity of cultural and social phenomena that has come to characterize an increasingly hybridized, post-industrial world" (p. 235). Another claim that Giroux makes for cultural studies is that it argues strongly that the role of media culture is central to understanding how power, privilege, and social desire intersect to structure daily life. As in other arenas of his work, Giroux is willing to nudge cultural studies to further its commitment to political work as a means of social reconstruction and progressive change.

Giroux also accepts the significance of media culture in structuring the daily life of a society. He believes that if we are to appreciate the value of cultural studies we must see the place of media culture in pedagogy. Following on this, Giroux would argue that educators go beyond transmitting fixed bodies of knowledge to critically examining "the problems of history, human agency, and the renewal of democratic public life" (Giroux, Larkshear, McLaren, and Peters, Eds., 1996, p. 46). In a very direct fashion, cultural studies can and should be linked with a critical pedagogy that questions the construction and use of knowledge, attitudes, values and social practices.

Cultural studies signified the refusal of a substantial fraction of a new generation of British and American intellectuals in the late 1950s and 1960s to observe the hierarchy between high culture and the culture of the popular classes. "The emergent discourses demanded the inclusion of women's, Third Worlds, and African-American writing, or alternatively, they claimed the irrelevance of the established canon in literature, philosophy, and criticism" (Giroux & Aronowitz, 1994, p. 173). As would be expected, this growing trend with its flourishing practices threatened the fortifications of the traditional canon and made those who wished to maintain control over institutional resources very nervous. In reality, cultural studies has forced a new worldview; a worldview that demands that categories of gender, race, and power be taken seriously. In its simplest terms, the battles within the academy are largely based around those who see knowledge as socially constructed and those who privilege expert or elite knowledge. One of the interesting aspects of the cultural studies movement has been its emerging influence on educational thought.

Race

Giroux contrasts this new racism to the old racism. He maintains "the old racism developed within the historical legacy of colonialism and modern slavery and rested on a blatant ideological appeal to pseudo-biological and scientific theories of race to justify inequality, hierarchies, and exploitation as part of the universal order" (1994, p. 74). Standing opposite to this view was the notion that whiteness represents itself as a universal marker for being civilized. This ideology leaves a lot of room for exclusion. Within both the old and the new forms of racism, there is little space to address the ethical and political aspects of the racist reality. Giroux understands the significance of race in the whole question of class politics; "class is actually lived through race." (2000, p. 28). Race is a hot political topic and can be viewed from many angles. "Scripted denials of racism coupled with the spectacle of racial discourse and representations have become a common occurrence in American life" (2004, p. 70).

Giroux believes that we are witnessing the emergence of a new racism. In *Disturbing Pleasures*, he claims that the New Right has developed a powerful new strategy for abstracting cultural difference from the discourse of democracy and social justice. This is done in a fashion that fuses nation, citizenship, and patriotism with a racially exclusive notion of difference. Giroux believes that "underlying the emergence of the new politics of racism and difference is a deep ambivalence on the part of liberals and conservatives about the traditional categories that have been used to defend racist practices" (1994, p. 75). It is no longer easy to maintain that white is right or that whiteness is synonymous with civilization itself. Now it seems necessary to invent new, if hegemonic, systems of racial superiority and subjugation. However, it must be admitted that such systems are anything but subtle.

Giroux sees that crime, in the form of community disorder and robbery has been identified as "an expression of black culture which in turn was defined as a cycle in which the negative effects of 'black matriarchy' and family pathology wrought destructive changes on the inner city by literally breeding deviancy out of deprivation and discrimination" (1994, p. 184). In *Channel Surfing*, Giroux expresses the belief that the attack on youth is linked to racism. "Racism feeds this attack on kids by targeting black youth as criminals while convincing working-class white youth that blacks and immigrants are responsible for the poverty, despair, and violence that have become a growing part of everyday life in American society" (1997b, p. 3). News reports often indicate to us that race is at the bottom of all our troubles. Giroux firmly believes that as a society we have reneged on our promise of social and economic mobility for the marginalized and disadvantaged. We do this in place of addressing the economic and political factors that undermine the possibility for a multiracial society and the formation of broad-based political coalitions. In the preface to *Channel Surfing*, Giroux walks through his own journey across race. In this way, he has found a potent way to remind us that the concerns of race are not just questions for somebody else. We all have these concerns and questions.

Giroux maintains that whiteness is no longer invisible. In fact it has become "a symbol of cultural identity and an object of critical scholarship, it has become both a symbol of resurgent racism and the subject of a rising academic specialization" (1997b, p. 89). Giroux goes on to claim that for conservative ideologues, whiteness has been appropriated as a badge of self-identity. The term has further been fashioned as a rallying point for disaffected whites who claim they are the victims of reverse racism in a country that is becoming increasingly racially diverse and hybridized. Now, like the neo-positivists, such whites feel besieged and persecuted. The other spin on this aspect of racism is the growing emphasis on what some have called whiteness studies. According to Giroux, this emerging area of scholarship has gathered a certain amount of media attention. This area of study is best known "for revealing how over time 'whiteness' in its various ideological and institutional forms has worked to perpetuate relations of domination and oppression against non-whites while simultaneously securing whites with a disproportionate amount of power and privilege" (1997b, p. 90). Giroux, true to form, sees the whole package as problematic. He believes that it is not enough to define whiteness as a form of domination and privilege. It is further necessary to provide a nuanced, dialectical, and layered account that would define whiteness largely as a form of domination. Such scholarship, while rightly unmasking whiteness as a mark of ideology and racial privilege, fails to provide a nuanced, dialectical, and layered account of whiteness that would allow appropriation as well as opposition. Giroux suggests that while we interrogate whiteness for its historical legacy "of racist exclusion and oppression, it is equally crucial that such work distinguish between 'whiteness' as a racial identity that is nonracist or antiracist and those aspects of 'whiteness' that are racist" (1997b, p. 91).

There is little doubt that race remains one of the most explosive issues of the day. The staggering images from New Orleans in the aftermath of Hurricane Katrina give new significance to the understandings put forward by writers like Henry Giroux. From Giroux's perspective, while the old racism unabashedly employed racist arguments in its endless quest for rationalizations and scapegoats,

> The new racism offers a two-pronged argumentation that, on the one hand, refuses to acknowledge that the issue of race is at the heart of its policymaking (as in welfare cutbacks, tougher crime bills and anti-immigration legislation) and, on the other hand, offers rationales for policy changes that claim to be color blind (as in the call to end affirmative action and racial gerrymandering). (1997b, p. 193)

This new racism, according to Giroux, works through the power of the judicial and legislative process. This process is legitimated and rationalized through the use of public intellectuals who often make racism seem respectable. Increasingly, the political podium, talk radio, national newspaper and magazines, and television have become the bully pulpits for the new racism.

Giroux contends that the "media culture is the central terrain on which the new racism has emerged. What counts as a source of education for many youth appears to reside in the spawning of electronic media, including radio talk shows, television, and film" (1996, p. 58). Giroux believes that given the ways in which racism and violence becomes part of a new aesthetic, it is crucial that educators and cultural workers find a means to put some form of assessment and balance into the picture. In a powerful chapter in the *Terror of Neoliberalism*, called "Spectacles of Race and Pedagogies of Denial," Giroux concludes that, "Any attempt to address the politics of the new racism . . . must begin by reclaiming the language of the social and affirming the project of an inclusive and just democracy" (2004, p. 75).

In *Fugitive Cultures*, Giroux writes that race is also connected to violence, and the violence is connected to pathology. "Real life and celluloid images blur as the representations of race and violence proliferate more broadly through the news media's extensive coverage of youth violence" (1996, p. 56). Giroux believes that when the discourse is racially coded it serves to mobilize white fears and allows calls for "drastic measures" to be raged into public policy. Legislation and the law step in to affirm the dominant. Then in the future, those who wish to exert their place will only have "to look to the law." This particular frightening circle of power completes itself.

Gender

This text is being written at a time when feminists, and other progressive groups, are being questioned and marginalized in universities. In the present time "the threat to academic freedom comes less from left-wing professors than it does from administrative demagogues and right-wing organizations willing to police and censor knowledge that does not silence itself before the legitimatizing imperatives of the traditional academic canon" (Giroux, 2000, p. 22). Given Giroux's overarching interest in the study of subjectivity, power, and pedagogy, it follows that he would become appreciative of the emerging work done by feminist writers. This fact becomes evident as we note the many feminist references he uses throughout his work. As with his other agendas, Giroux searches for the political in feminist thinking and action. He realizes that a central point in the feminist movement has been the important concept that the personal is political. Giroux further insists that the problematizing of gender relations represents a crucial contribution made by feminists. He claims that this has been done, in large part, by indicating how "women are inscribed in patriarchal representations and relations of power, but also on how gender relations can be used to problematize the sexual identities, differences, and commonalities of both men and women" (1997a, p. 208).

Giroux believes that feminist theorists have done much to redefine the relationship between the personal and the political, in ways that go beyond the implications for gender concerns, to advance more global postmodern assumptions. Giroux believes that this redefinition has come from "a growing feminist criticism that rejects the notions that sexuality is the only axis of domination and that the study of sexuality should be limited theoretically to an exclusive focus on how women's subjectivities are constructed" (1997a, p. 209). When Giroux writes in this fashion he helps us better realize the value and power of feminist thought. In this way he extends the borders of feminism beyond social category, and attempts to counteract the "culture of corporate public pedagogy [that] largely cancels out or devalues gender, class-specific, and racial injustices of the existing social order" (2004, p. 106).

However, here as elsewhere Giroux is not hesitant to bring a critical lens to his examination and use of feminism. He realizes that while it is necessary to name the pain and the blame, it is not enough to stay at that level of critical encounter. Beyond the pain and the blame there must be a place of possibility. Central to any critical approach to subjectivity, power, and pedagogy there must be a transformative moment. Such transformative moments are to be found in a reflective encounter grounded in context and specificity. Otherwise we are left making totalizing, essentialist, and possibly, politically repressive claims. Giroux writes: "Postmodern feminism recognizes that we need a notion of large narratives that privileges forms of analyses in which it is possible to make visible those mediations, interrelations, and interdependencies that give shape and power to larger political and social systems" (1997a, p. 212).

Giroux has done us a stellar service by examining how the most salient concepts used in feminism contribute to our greater understanding of social forms and human agency. For example, he has pointed out that postmodern feminism, in particular, has done much to frame the whole issue of difference. The notion of difference is a crucial topic for emancipatory pedagogy. In addition to this, Giroux gives credit to feminists for further developing the notion of difference as a political factor in postmodern thought.

Giroux, even in his earliest work, was quite interested in the power of social institutions to promote sex-role socialization. However, even then he knew that it was too simplistic to merely name and blame. He knew that simply exposing the gender-based stereotypes found in school practices would not be enough to solve the concerns and problems locked to gender discrimination. He, like others, realized that we must consider the issue of how the gender relations presented and legitimated in schools benefit both men and women and the interests and needs of capital. Further to that, Giroux noted the need to provide an historical analysis of how and why gender relations have taken different forms, and how sexism gets sedimented in personality structures. In *Postmodernism, Feminism, and Cultural Politics*, Giroux claims that:

> Feminist theory has always engaged in a dialectical relationship with modernism. On the one hand, it has stressed modernist concerns with equality, social justice, and freedom through an ongoing engagement with substantive political issues. On the other hand, postmodern feminism has rejected those aspects of modernism in which universal laws are exalted at the expense of specificity and contingency. (1991, p. 31)

As stated above, Giroux has done much to indicate the place of feminism in the postmodern world. In particular, he realizes that postmodern feminism opposes any linear view of history that props up the traditional patriarchal notions of subjectivity and society. He further points out that postmodern feminism rejects the notion that truth and objectivity are the sole domains of science and reason. He goes on to say that in fact postmodern feminism rejects the black and white way we view modernism and postmodernism. Giroux acknowledges that postmodern feminism would instead wish to construct a feminist political project that would make use of both worldviews. "Central to the notion of critical pedagogy is a politics of voice that combines a postmodern notion of difference with a feminist emphasis on the primacy of the political" (1997a, p. 224). For Giroux this approach means that we need to pay more attention to the personal and realize that as people we are constructed in multiple and complex ways. As educators we need to affirm this diversity and acknowledge how identities are part of our social, cultural, and institutional settings. With this mind-set we can help our students understand themselves and the world around them. The contribution of feminist thought here is to underscore the fact that students have multiple identities, and that they will connect with the large world in their own fashion.

Giroux claims that the contribution made by postmodern feminism includes providing a model of the most progressive aspects of modernism and postmodernism. "In the most general sense, it reaffirms the importance of difference as part of a broader political struggle for the reconstruction of public life. It rejects all forms of essentialism but recognizes the importance of certain formative narratives" (1993, p. 71). Further to this, postmodern feminism offers a language of power that engages the issue of inequality and struggle. This is a crucial contribution, not only for understanding gender relations, but also for interrogating other social realities. Postmodern feminism, as far as Giroux is concerned, has also given us a language that helps us penetrate the ambiguous connections between human agency and structured institutions. It provides a radical social theory imbued with a language of critique and possibility. That is quite a contribution.

Reading Reality

Ideology

One of the greatest accomplishments of critical pedagogy and cultural studies has been to help unmask the pervasive presence of ideology in our social settings and institutions. To this day many universities, schools, museums, and prisons claim to operate as if such social sites are not ideological. In the process of schooling and education, understanding how ideology operates helps explain why actors take on certain roles, why given policies are approved, why a limited curriculum is accepted, and why questionable practices are perpetuated. We all operate out of ideologies. We all say and do what we genuinely believe is best. We all would pass the ideological lie-detector test. In fact it is not easy to see through our own ideologies. However, accepting that we think, speak, and act out of taken-for-granted ideologies is a crucial reflective step towards transforming our local schooling and educational sites. As Henry Giroux states:

> Ideology is a crucial construct for understanding how meaning is produced, transformed, and consumed by individuals and social groups. As a tool of critical analysis, it digs beneath the phenomenal forms of classroom knowledge and social practices and helps to locate the structuring principles and ideas that mediate between the dominant society and the everyday experiences of teachers and students. (1997a, p. 91)

Giroux talks about ideology as "a dynamic construct that refers to the ways in which meanings are produced, mediated, and embodied in knowledge forms, social practices, and cultural experiences" (1988a, p. 5). Ideology can be seen not only as a set of doctrines but also as a medium through which we can make sense of our lives. According to Giroux, ideology is useful in helping us understand how schools, for example, produce and sustain meanings. This, to us, seems to be a powerful critical tool. Through the use of such a tool, educators can examine the current values and practices that are part of our educational sites.

Giroux realizes that as educators we must appreciate the reality of ideology, if we are to deal seriously with the issues of agency, struggle, and critique. Even in his earliest writings, Giroux realized that the relationship between ideology and schooling was problematic. As Giroux attempted to "broaden the parameters of how we think about schooling, education, pedagogy, and cultural practices" (1993, p. 2), he brought with him the significant conceptual tool of ideology. Of course it is much more than a theoretical tool. Giroux is quite aware of this: "The complexity of the concept is captured in the notion that while ideology is an active process involving the production, consumption, and representation of meaning and behavior, it cannot be reduced to either consciousness or a system of practices . . ." (1997a, p. 75). Giroux tells us that the character of ideology is dialectical. He goes on to remind us that ideology can illuminate the relationships among power, meaning, and interest. An examination of these issues "provides a theoretical grounding for interrogating the issue of how ideology is inscribed in those forms of educational discourse through which school experiences and practices are ordered and constituted" (2005b, p. 116). We know that these relationships are ever present in the daily living of schooling and education. Such relationships are often masked under the regimes of commonsense, tradition, and the natural. Therefore the exposure of such relationships is crucial if we are to transform particular sites of schooling and education. For example, Giroux would have us develop course objectives that go beyond the limitations of the humanistic and behavioral objectives schools. He believes that the starting point for such objectives would be to view educational knowledge as a study in ideology. In this way, educators would raise questions about the so-called shared assumptions that are buried in the curriculum. From Giroux's perspective, we need to appreciate the ideological links between socially constructed knowledge and classroom learning. We try to do this in our teaching.

In another instance, Giroux helps us understand the significance of ideology by claiming, "the making of citizens must be understood as an ideological process through which we experience ourselves as well as our relations to others and the world within a complex and often contradictory system of representations and images" (2005b, p. 16). In relation to this question, Giroux believes we need to go beyond simply analyzing the interests underlying particular forms of knowledge. In fact, we need to critically examine the issue of how ideology functions through the organization of images, space, and time, to construct a particular kind of social subject. He does this most persuasively in his comments about neoliberalism. "Neoliberalism is not simply an economic policy designed to cut government spending, pursue free-trade policies, and free market forces from government regulations, it is also a political philosophy and ideology that affects every dimension of social life" (2004, p. 52). Any conceptual tool that can help us to better do such a task has to be of great value. Giroux has done much to help educators and cultural workers understand, appreciate, and use the conceptual tool of ideology.

Pedagogy

As indicated by Kincheloe, McLaren and Steinberg, Giroux's work in the 1990s has done much to reestablish the place of pedagogy in the wider sphere of cultural studies. For them, as for Giroux, pedagogy "involves the production and transmission of knowledge, the construction of subjectivity, and the learning of values and beliefs." (Giroux, 1997a, p. xiii). In many ways this reemphasis brings Giroux back to his roots. His earlier work focused, in large part, on developing a sense of pedagogy. One of Giroux's strongest insights was that pedagogy could not be seen or treated as an isolated aspect of life. "Pedagogy merges politics and ethics with revitalized forms of civic education that provide the knowledge, skills, and experiences enabling individual freedom and social agency" (2003c). By his own admission Giroux initially believed that pedagogy was a discipline developed around the narrow imperatives of public schooling. He believed this while realizing that his own identity was largely formed outside of school. Like many of us, he now more fully realizes that films, books, journals, videos, and music did more to shape his politics and life than did any formal education. Like many of our own students, he traditionally saw schooling as being about somebody else's dreams. Of course, any discourse about identity is always contingent upon an analysis of history and power. Now Giroux is more interested in arguing that a critical public pedagogy needs to help "make visible alternative models of radical democratic relations in a wide variety of sites" (2004, p. 138).

Giroux realizes that in most discourses, pedagogy is often treated as a discrete set of strategies and skills that are used to teach prescribed subject matter. "Pedagogy as a critical practice in which students learn to be attentive and responsible to the memoirs and narratives of others disappears within the corporate and test-driven learning" (2003a, p. 87). In this way the notion of pedagogy is limited to content, method, and resources and is often devoid of necessary questions surrounding knowledge, authority, and power. Beyond this, "pedagogy is implicated in the construction and organization of knowledge, desires, values, and social practices" (Giroux, 1994, p. 64-65). From this perspective, Giroux developed an ever-expanding notion of critical pedagogy. This work, done in comradeship with Peter McLaren, Roger Simon, Stanley Aronowitz and others, has become a central pillar of educational thought and practice.

In time, Giroux began to doubt that "pedagogy as a form of political, moral, and social production can be addressed primarily as a matter of schooling" (1993, p. 1). In fact what grew out of this doubt was a highly developed concept of border pedagogy. In many ways the notion of border pedagogy has forced us to rethink our whole approach to education. For Giroux, the category of border signals a recognition of the epistemological, political, cultural, and social margins that structure the language of history, power, and difference. This is a powerful insight when it comes to examining the place of pedagogy in our educational institutions. It follows from this that as educators we need to be concerned with finding ways of crossing such borders. Giroux claims that it is crucial for us to challenge and redefine such borders. He goes on to say that it is essential to create pedagogical conditions in which students become border crossers. In this way they can better understand otherness in its own terms. It can be said that our understanding of otherness and difference are essential to any critical pedagogy.

Giroux believes that "the concept of border pedagogy makes visible the historically and socially constructed strengths and limitations of those places and borders we inherit and that frame our discourses and social relations" (1993, p. 28). In relation to a border pedagogy, Giroux places emphasis on the political and the ethical. He stresses that we need to work on the political front by examining how institutions, knowledge, and social relations are inscribed in a nexus of power. He would highlight the ethical by examining how the shifting relations of knowing, acting, and subjectivity are constructed in cultural spaces and social relationships. Giroux is wise in reminding us that "pedagogical practices operate within institutional contexts that carry great power in determining which knowledge is of most worth, what it means for students to know something, and how such knowledge relates to a particular understanding of the self and its relationship to both others and the future" (2003c).

In many ways the notion of border pedagogy is an added frame for the further development of a critical pedagogy. Border pedagogy can be seen as an evolution and refinement of Giroux's earlier work on pedagogy. Like most of Giroux's writing we cannot read border pedagogy, critical pedagogy, or pedagogy as discrete concepts. It is for that reason that we have treated these three aspects of pedagogy under one heading. Giroux sees pedagogy as a central aspect of cultural practice and warns us to use this concept with respectful caution. "Pedagogy as a mode of witnessing, a public space in which students learn to be attentive and responsible to the memories and narratives of others" (Giroux & Myrsiades, Eds., 2001, p. 8). In a cogent comment about critical pedagogy, he writes that while there is no generic definition, there are important theoretical insights and practices that can be found in many of the approaches to critical pedagogy. Giroux believes that these insights often circumscribe a set of educational problems. Such problems "include but are not limited to the relationships between knowledge and power, language and experience, ethics and authority, student agency and transformative politics, and teacher location and student formations" (1997a, p. 168).

In his earliest writings, Giroux saw that pedagogy was presented in an atheoretical, ahistorical, and unproblematic fashion. Giroux, never encumbered by subtlety, pointedly claims that it is important to reveal "the myths, lies, and injustices at the heart of the dominant school culture" (1988a, p. 7). Giroux calls for a mode of dialogue and critique that unmasks the dominant school culture's attempt to escape from history. Along with this critical attitude, he would have educators examine the assumptions and practices that are part of day-to-day schooling. Teachers and parents need to see knowledge as socially constructed and therefore subject to the going ideological interests. Knowledge is neither neutral nor objective. "Knowledge must be linked to the issue of power, which suggests that educators and others must raise questions about its truth claims as well as the interests that such knowledge serves" (pp. 7–8).

Giroux is also interested in understanding how "representations are constructed as a means of comprehending the past through the present in order to legitimate and secure a particular view of the future" (Giroux & McLaren 1994, p. 47). He has pedagogical motives behind this particular quest. Namely, how do students learn to make sense of their worlds by examining the various representational images they encounter? Giroux would have us, and our students, demystify these identity representations by peeling back the layers of formative "history, social forms, and modes of ethical address" that are so often taken as neutral. He goes on to warn us, that behind these representations are, "forms of textual authority and relations of power" (p. 47) that shape the very face of our living. To counter this Giroux would encourage pedagogy of representation that looks beyond the images, sounds, and texts to probe the construction of the knowledge we use and the identities we "inherit."

Giroux seems to have always realized that for pedagogy to be radical, it needed to combine the language of critique with the language of possibility. For him, it was never enough to simply critique; it was also crucial to encourage transformation. Pedagogy needs to be positioned in a political sphere for, as Giroux claims, it represents a struggle to define and is itself a struggle over power relations. "Making the pedagogical more political means inserting schooling directly into the political sphere by arguing that schooling represents both a struggle to define meaning and a struggle over power relations" (1988a, p. 127). The agenda here, as far as Giroux is concerned, is to help students develop an active sense of the struggle to overcome economic, political, and social injustices. Giroux consistently talks about making the political more pedagogical. This is done, he maintains, by utilizing forms of pedagogy that embody political interests that are emancipatory in nature. Giroux is most helpful and succinct when he writes, "critical pedagogy is grounded in a sense of history, politics, and ethics which uses theory as a resource to respond to particular contexts, problems, and issues" (2003, p. 18). Following on this lead means treating students as critical agents, making knowledge problematic, utilizing critical and affirming dialogue, and making the case for a better world for all. The second part of this book describes selected efforts to do this.

Students need to have a sense of alternative possibilities. This has to be done against a backdrop of examining individual lives against the constraints and possibilities of the wider society. To do this, critical pedagogy needs to be lived as a form of cultural practice. This goes beyond telling students how to think. Students need to be helped to produce rather than simply accept knowledge. Of course this is not easy for us as educators. We have been trained to be the ones who know. One of the most important aspects of Giroux's contribution to educational thought is his assertion that pedagogy functions not only to transmit knowledge but to produce knowledge. "As a historical construct, critical pedagogy functions in a dual sense to address the issue of what kinds of knowledge can be put in place that enable rather than subvert the formation of a democratic society" (1993, p. 101).

It was in an effort to rethink the relations between the centers and the margins of power that Giroux developed the notion of border pedagogy. Basic to such a development is the appreciation that the texts of various media are social and historical constructions. "Border pedagogy also stresses that students must be provided with the opportunity to critically engage the strengths and limitations of the cultural and social codes that define their own histories and narratives" (1993b, p. 136). In order to do this, students need to function as border-crossers. We have to remember that there are not only physical borders, but cultural borders as well. These borders have been historically constructed and socially organized. Such constructing and organizing serve, as far as Giroux is concerned, to either limit or enable particular identities, individual capacities, and social form. It seems to follow that we can only learn if we are willing to cross the borders of accepted knowledge that are often fenced by experience and tradition. These cultural, social, and historical places are rarely fixed.

In following the invites of border pedagogy, Giroux claims that it is not enough for teachers to merely affirm uncritically their students' histories, experiences, and stories. These histories, experiences, and stories cannot simply be taken at face value. They need to be critically examined and put into their historical and social frames. "Such a process involves more than allowing students to speak from their own histories and social formations. It also raises questions about how teachers use power to cross borders that are culturally strange to them" (1993, p. 141).

One of Giroux's agenda items is that we as educators get beyond the demand for linking theoretical text with specific classroom practices. Of course this is not easy, for the preoccupation is with very practical methods, content, and resources. If we are to get beyond being educational technicians, we need to see "pedagogy as a configuration of textual, verbal, and visual practices that seek to engage the processes through which people understand themselves and the ways in which they engage others and their environment" (1993, p. 3).

Giroux writes that as a form of cultural production, "pedagogy takes on the goal of challenging canonicity and interrogating the forms of exclusion and inclusion in the production, distribution, and circulation of knowledge" (Giroux & Shannon, 1997, p. 5). In a practical way, Giroux sees pedagogy as the place where students critically engage and challenge the diverse cultural discourses, practices, and popular media that surround them. Giroux, throughout his writings, reminds us that our understanding of pedagogy needs to be expanded beyond the limited emphasis on the mastery of techniques and methodologies.

In *Popular Culture, Schooling and Everyday Life*, Giroux and Simon argue that pedagogy is usually treated in one of two ways: as a method or as a process. They claim that, "what is often ignored is the notion of pedagogy as a cultural production and exchange that addresses how knowledge is produced, mediated, refused, and re-presented within relations of power both in and outside of schooling" (1989, p. 2). It is crucial to recognize the importance of what happens outside of schools. It can be said that students get their sense of identity, politics, and culture from other personal and social sites that might not be connected to school in any significant fashion. It seems absurd to teach as if these other sites were not crucial to students' formation, yet we often ask students, by the very way we use curriculum, to leave their beliefs, values, and experiences at the school door.

As far as Giroux is concerned, pedagogy must be seen as a form of cultural politics and as a form of cultural production. "Pedagogy is a deliberate attempt to influence how and what knowledge and identities are produced within and among particular sets of social relations" (Giroux & Simon, 1989, p. 222). Pedagogy draws attention to the processes through which knowledge is produced. This is a concise and an important point. Pedagogy "includes the integration in practice of particular curriculum content and design, classroom strategies and techniques, a time and space for the practice of the strategies and techniques, and evaluation purposes and methods" (p. 222). Giroux and Simon point out that pedagogy does more than this: there is the question of what knowledge is of most worth, what we should desire, and how we represent others and ourselves. Pedagogy then, is about the practice of teaching and learning, plus the cultural politics that stand behind such practice. In this book we contextualize and describe our practices of teaching and learning. That is our pedagogical project here.

Giroux, like his colleague Roger Simon, uses pedagogy in an expanded and politicized fashion. They both believe that in doing pedagogy, it is necessary to name and problematize the social relations, experiences, and ideologies that are active in a given site. For them, such sites are not limited to schools and other official educational institutions, but may include such diverse places as families, churches, community groups, labor organizations, businesses, and local media. It follows that in our school and university practice, we remember that pedagogy is happening around us and that students bring pedagogy with them. Giroux and Simon believe that critical pedagogy should begin with "a degree of indignation, a vision of possibility, and an uncertainty: it demands that we constantly rethink and renew the work we have done as part of a wider theory of schooling as a form of cultural politics" (1989, p. 233).

As Giroux and Aronowitz acknowledge in *Education Still Under Siege*, the starting point for a critical education would have been Paulo Freire's notion "that the form and content of knowledge, as well as the social practices through which it is appreciated, have to be seen as part of an ongoing struggle over what counts as legitimate culture and forms of empowerment" (1993, p. 151). Giroux and Aronowitz would have critical pedagogy stress forms of language and knowledge that would help provide a critical understanding of how social reality works. They believe that it is not wise to simply reject dominant ideologies but rather challenge and critically appropriate them.

A critical pedagogy needs to take the historical and social particularities of students' experiences as a starting point and then go on to examine them in a critical fashion. Once again, Giroux and Aronowitz stress that it is not enough to simply debunk existing forms of schooling and educational theory. We have been there and have done that. Now, in a process of educational evolution, we need to build on the democratic possibilities that are inherent in our schools, pedagogy, and theory.

This process is helped if we see pedagogy itself as representing an act of production. Giroux claims that teachers and students produce knowledge in their very interaction with a text. Knowledge is also produced in an interpretative practice when texts are read as part of a wider set of cultural and historical experiences. When teachers and students, with different sets of attitudes, values, and experiences, take up such texts knowledge is produced. Following this logic, it is easier to see that pedagogy, like knowledge, is a historical construction. In this way, pedagogy is bound up in economic, social, and political practices that are produced in particular sets of social relations. For Giroux, the pedagogical stress should not be on getting the right answer, but to be able to reason through different presented meanings. Pedagogy needs to be that place to deal with "the views and problems that deeply concern students in their everyday lives" (Giroux & McLaren, 1989, p. 150). Giroux, however, is too experienced a teacher to advocate that the curriculum agenda would be limited to such content. Elsewhere we have written about our attempts to bring about change at the level of the individual because we are interested in encouraging our students, in a downsized academic unit, to become transformative intellectuals, cultural workers, and democratic leaders. We carry on this work here.

Reading Promise

Curriculum

From the beginning of his public writings, Giroux was suspicious of the way that curriculum development, design, and evaluation were guided by the dictates of the "real" world. This was done, he believed, at the expense of educational theory. "Central to this form of rationality in the curriculum field is the notion of objectivity and neutrality. Guided by the search for reliability, consistency, and quantitative predictions, positivist educational practice excludes the role of values, feelings, and subjectivity defined meaning . . ." (1981, p. 1). Of course, since Giroux wrote *Ideology, Culture, and the Process of Schooling,* many researchers have come to accept the value of narrative criteria and the place of subjective data in our search to better understand the goals of curriculum. In our graduate research work, we make use of narrative criteria as well as subjective data. For many of our students, these criteria and this form of data are the most informative. However, this does not mean that we are out of the positivist woods. As we have stated elsewhere in this book, positivist thought is very much alive and is galloping through our educational institutions. Giroux believes that beneath the positivist educational agenda lurks a conservative ideology that needs to be exposed. It is not hard to see how such an agenda, where it is dominant, has tremendous influence on what information and knowledge gets selected and affirmed in schools and other educational institutions. Invariably, this selection and affirmation is bound up with control and power. Here it is important to remember, "power relations exist in correlation with forms of school knowledge that both distort the truth and produce it" (1997b, p. 108).

Giroux believes that it is necessary for curriculum to consistently renew itself. He emphasizes the need for a self-critical approach that understands "the interface of ideology, dominant institutional interests, and curriculum theory" (1981, p. 113). One of the tools, Giroux claims, for such a self-critical approach is the concept of praxis. One of the ways that Giroux uses the concept praxis is to see it as the transition from critical thought to reflective intervention. We believe that part of our own agenda in working with graduate and undergraduate students is to help them realize that much of their work is or can be a form of praxis. It is much too easy for teachers and professors, caught in the vice of time, to accept the invitations of prepackaged curriculum text and material in order to deliver the content expected of them. In our discussion about teachers we have indicated how this practice can turn them into glorified educational technicians.

One of the tenets of Giroux's thought about curriculum has to do with the need to place students at the center of the learning process. In order to do this teachers and professors would need to take seriously those cultural experiences and meanings "that students bring to the day-to-day process of schooling itself. If we take the experiences of our students as a starting point for dialogue and analysis, we give them the opportunity to validate themselves, to use their own voices" (1981, p. 123). This suggestion is in stark contrast to "a predetermined and hierarchically arranged body of knowledge [that] is taken as the cultural currency to be dispensed to all children regardless of their diversity and interests" (p. 123). When the school curriculum is built around such a body of knowledge, teachers are often left in the trap of having to expend much of their energy on controlling and managing students.

There is a very wide scope open to us as we examine Giroux's discussion on curriculum. Our experience indicates that one of the most interesting topics for graduate students seems to be the hidden curriculum. We believe that one of the reasons for this interest is that dealing with this topic, in all its manifestations, allows a person to look at education in a fresh way. Very often students who are open to interrogating education and the practices of schooling are surprised by what they find. Of course, those who are steeped in neo-positivist thought often deny the existence of any hidden curriculum. As far as they are concerned, knowledge is objective and neutral and therefore there is nothing hidden about it.

Giroux wrote extensively about the hidden curriculum in his earlier work. As usual, he did not take this concept for granted, but brought his formidable critical lens to the task of examining the very concept of hidden curriculum. However, he realized what a valuable conceptual tool the hidden curriculum was for understanding the complexity of education and schooling. The concept of the hidden curriculum allows us to make "linkages between schools and the social, economic, and political landscape that make up the wider society, the hidden curriculum theorists provided a theoretical impetus for breaking out of the methodological quagmire in which schools were merely viewed as black boxes" (1983, p. 45). In writing about the hidden curriculum, Giroux spelled out a number of important insights that hold real value for us as educators. These insights hinge on the claims that: schools need to be analyzed in their socioeconomic context; schools are political sites; and the commonsense values and beliefs that guide classroom practice are social constructions. These insights remain as grounding tenets for critical pedagogy. They greatly influence our work.

As Giroux points out, the concept of the hidden curriculum has received conflicting definitions and analyses. However, the basic claim for the hidden curriculum centers on "those unstated norms, values, and beliefs embedded in and transmitted to students through the underlying rules that structure the routines and social relationships in school and classroom life" (1983, p. 47). Giroux would have our work on the hidden curriculum be much more than description. He would have us go on to critique the social reality that allows and drives a hidden curriculum. This means, in part, getting at the ideological assumptions that are part of the case being examined. Giroux further claims that the concept of the hidden curriculum needs to become a central issue in the development of curriculum theory. It follows that the concept of the hidden curriculum be used as a transformative tool. In other words, once we realize that there are elements of a hidden curriculum lurking in our practice, we need to do something about it.

In many ways, school curriculum is the means by which many ideological and special interest groups try to exert their influence. It is interesting how many such ideological groups publicly devalue schools yet they want to control the agenda of such schools. Giroux writes:

> Since the early 1980s, big business has attempted to play a vital role in redefining the purpose and meaning of public schooling. Rejecting a concern with issues of equity, racial justice, sexual equality, and cultural democracy, conservatives have reasserted the debate over making schools relevant to students' lives by reducing the curriculum to little more than job preparation. (1994, p. 48)

As far as Giroux is concerned, this is tantamount to educating the vast majority of students for a type of functional literacy that prepares them for specialized employment and efficient consumption. We have to realize that when many employers complain about the poor quality of students from the public school systems, technical colleges, and universities they really are simply commenting on the graduates' use-value to them.

Giroux has consistently maintained that curriculum must not be the caged domain of the few and the privileged, but it must center on the "particular forms of life, culture, and interaction that students bring to school" (2005b, p. 104). In another place Giroux writes, "critical pedagogy always strives to incorporate student experience as official curriculum content. While articulating such experience can be both empowering and a form of critique against relations that silence, such experience is not an unproblematic form of knowledge" (Giroux & Simon, 1989, p. 231). Giroux suggests, "instead of stressing the individualistic and competitive approaches to learning, students are encouraged to work together on projects, both in terms of their production and evaluation" (2005b, p. 104). Over the past decade many teachers and university professors have learned to attempt and accomplish such work. Like Giroux, we realize that the experience of students' lives is not quite enough to build a curriculum around. Students need to expand their boundaries and borders "while constantly pushing them to test what it means to resist oppression, work collectively, and exercise authority from the position of an ever-developing sense of knowledge, expertise, and commitment" (p. 104). This is a powerful claim for curriculum and pedagogy.

It is helpful to ask the Giroux questions: How can we celebrate personal experience while nudging students to go beyond what they already know? How can students' previous experience be both acknowledged and challenged? How can we affirm student voices while encouraging the interrogation of such voices? How can students be encouraged to hear the voices of others? These are crucial questions, and they are questions that help us shape our practical curriculum work with students. By being aware of such critical questions we can temper our daily work with students in a fashion that goes beyond transmission to touch on transformation.

Giroux proposes that we need to rethink the very nature of curriculum theory. He believes that to do so it is necessary to: expand the notion of the political; link the languages of critique and possibility; view teachers as public intellectuals; and reformulate the relationship between theory and practice. Part of this quest begins with making school knowledge problematic. That is, we need to ask: What counts as school knowledge? How is school knowledge organized? What underlying codes structure school knowledge? How is school knowledge transmitted? How is school knowledge accessed? What cultural system does school knowledge legitimate? and Whose interests are served by this school knowledge? These salient questions grew out of the new sociology of education movement in England, but have been harnessed and sharpened by educational theorists such as Henry Giroux. In fact, if we keep such questions before us as we teach, we are bound to temper our pedagogy in a way that helps our students to be more critical as well as empowered with regard to their own teaching.

It is our belief that some of the more interesting theoretical breakthroughs in education, over the past two decades, have come in the field of curriculum. However, it does not follow that we, in an educational community, always act as if there has been such an evolution. We constantly see central offices of education packaging curricula for universal dissemination. This is more so today with the emphasis on standardization. What we need instead, according to Giroux and Aronowitz, is "really useful knowledge that draws from popular education, knowledge that challenges and critically appropriates dominant ideologies, and knowledge that points to more human and democratic social relations and cultural forms" (1994, p. 153). For Giroux and Aronowitz, it is important for students to master language and to have the capacity to think conceptually and critically.

Those who read only the back covers of Giroux's books may miss the point that he struggles not simply to debunk existing forms of schooling, curriculum, and educational theory, but to rework such forms in a way that both contests and appropriates. And out of that struggle comes a new production. This, for us, is a true critical process.

Higher Education

One of the things that Henry Giroux does really well is to put his claims, probes, and perspectives in their wider context. In a recent writing he is acutely aware that the recent attacks on education, "especially in light of the growing corporatization and privatization at all levels of schooling, is a refusal on the part of many theorists to rethink the role academics might play in defending the university as a crucial democratic public sphere" (2000, p. 17). Part of our own agenda in this book is to suggest ways of working in the university as if it is a crucial democratic public sphere. Beliefs about higher education range from the proposition that the university represents a new form of cultural bar-

barism to the claim that the university is intellectually dead. Of course the belief systems surrounding the university in general have a real impact on the
prevailing view of institutions that offer teacher education. This is especially
true if the claim is that university academics have no role as critical public intellectuals. This is not easy with the growing trends toward corporatization in
universities. "Reducing higher education to the handmaiden of corporate culture works against the critical social imperative of educating citizens who can
sustain and develop inclusive democratic public spheres" (Giroux & Myrsiades, 2001, p. 33). In a real sense this cuts right through any critical pedagogy
agenda. Much of the foundation for critical pedagogy's agenda is based on the
call for educators to be public intellectuals. The attacks on the university "are
part of a broader attack on the regime of political democracy itself" (Giroux &
Giroux, 2004, p. 46). We know first hand from our work in academics that
similar ideological battles are raging in universities. This is especially true now
that the neopositivists have come to realize the academic capital they have lost
to their more liberated colleagues, as well as the status they have lost in the
minds of their students. Therefore, the struggle for a critical agenda, whatever
frame it might take, has to be fought both inside, as well as outside, the university. However, Susan Giroux and Henry Giroux are realistic in their views
about the struggle. "The assumption that education alone can alter iniquitous
social conditions is both unrealistic and naive in that it depicts how such institutions are affected by those political and economic conditions that they are
allegedly supposed to counter" (p. 51).

Giroux believes that a "new regimen of teacher training would have to be
instituted to replace the 'methods' taught in many teacher colleges. Teachers
would be encouraged to become intellectuals in the technical sense; that is, to
attain a degree of mastery over the legacy of high culture as well as assimilate
and validate the elements of students' experience, which is intimately bound
with popular culture" (Giroux & Aronowitz, 1994, p. 154). Giroux also adds a
cautionary vote about the significance of online education. The reality is that
more and more of our universities and high schools are part of the mechanisms of the great World Wide Web. For purposes of convenience for our
students, and resources for our institutions distance learning has become an
accepted fixture. In fact it has become a fixture to boast about. It is our belief
and experience that this aspect of school and university learning needs to be
treated in a critical fashion. Possibly, we do not want to see what might be under that microscope. When the social becomes digital then we need to exam-

ine the significance of such practices in light of the "need to reclaim the meaning and purpose of secondary education as an ethical and political response to the demise of democratic public life" (2003c).

While we have dealt with some aspects of Giroux's understanding of cultural studies elsewhere, it is worth restating that he puts great stock in the potential contribution it has for education. Giroux believes that cultural studies broadens our understanding of how politics and power work through institutions, language, representations, and culture. As far as Giroux is concerned, one of the strongest contributions cultural studies makes to education is in raising questions about how culture is related to power and the politics of representation. Giroux also believes that we need to redefine the meaning of public intellectuals to a position as "critical citizens whose collective knowledge and actions presuppose specific visions of public life, community, and moral accountability" (Giroux & Shannon, 1997, p 8).

Giroux stresses that the process of educational reform needs to get beyond the narrow technocratic models that presently dominate discussions. "Hence, the regulation, certification, and standardization of teacher behavior is emphasized over creating conditions for teachers to undertake the sensitive political and ethical roles they might assume as public intellectuals educating students for responsible, critical citizenship" (Giroux & Shannon, 1997, p. 232). This total view is contaminated by claims to being professional, scientific, and objective. Once again the positivist imperative is at work. In addition to this reality, faculties and colleges of education are aligned along subject specific, disciplinary, or administrative categories. This allows little opportunity for students and instructors to study and teach in multidisciplinary settings. Of course this very structure is heavy with messages about knowledge; how it gets constructed, managed, and delivered.

Cultural studies theorists argue that pedagogy as it is practiced in schools and universities is much more than a set of techniques and skills. Pedagogy is "a cultural practice that can be understood only through considerations of history, politics, power, and culture" (Giroux & Shannon, 1997, p. 233). Giroux contends that in the future, the meaning and purpose of schooling, what it means to teach, and how students should be taught to live in a global, high tech, and racially diverse world, must be addressed. One of the ways to begin answering some of these questions is to analyze "the full range of assorted and densely layered sites of learning such as the media, popular culture, film, advertising, mass communications, and religious organizations" (p. 235) in a fashion that extends what we normally see as school learning.

We believe, following on Giroux's lead, that professors in faculties of education need to see themselves not merely as professional academics but as citizens who have a democratic vision and sense of community responsibility. As academics we are not always ready to respond to this invitation because, in part, it takes us out of our comfortable place. Traditionally teacher education programs have been "dominated by their behavioristic orientation towards the issues of mastery and methodological refinement as the basis for developing teacher competence" (Giroux & Aronowitz, 1994, p. 36). In such a view teachers are not seen as creative and imaginative thinkers who can get beyond methods and critically evaluate the significance of their work. In fact, many present-day teacher evaluation practices are replete with questions concerning the dutiful fulfillment of the dictates of others, the implementation of pre-packaged curricula, and the standards achieved. We have found in our own endeavors at reforming teacher education that the struggles between the expert model and the transformative model are blatant. Giroux and Aronowitz, writing in *Education Still Under Siege*, would have us "educate students to be teacher-scholars by developing educational courses that focus on the immediacy of school problems and substitute the discourse of management and efficiency for a critical analysis of the underlying conditions that structure school life" (p. 36). As will become evident in the second part of this book, *Teaching Giroux*, it is not always easy to make this leap. Yet, as teacher educators, we must not fall into the binary trap of teaching solely for the practical or solely for the theoretical.

Teachers need to be able to ponder over such questions as: What counts as knowledge? What is worth teaching? What is the purpose and nature of instruction? and What is the school's role in society? These are not questions for "someone else," they are the intellectual concerns of all of us. If we are not encouraged and helped to deal with such questions, then the practical outcome will be that our graduating teachers can only be educational technicians.

Teacher education students, both at the undergraduate and graduate levels, need to realize that excellence is more complex than high reading or math scores. In this day of accountability and standards there is tremendous pressure for teachers to "give in," to "simply get the job done," and to hope that students "measure up." The ideology that sits under this management pedagogy is crippling to the notion of teachers as intellectuals. It seems crucial that teacher education programs have to fly beyond the dominant management pedagogy and help transform our own places of work.

From Giroux's earliest writings we see that he realized "the dialectical tension that exists between teacher-education programs and the dominant society through a set of concepts that link as well as demonstrate the interplay of power, ideology, biography, and history" (1981, p. 143). Giroux sees that teacher-education programs are caught in a "deceptive paradox." Faculties of education are expected to educate teachers to help generations of students have the knowledge and skills to live in a democratic society. At the same time such faculties constitute a powerful agency for representing that society, with all its inequalities and promise. This paradox remains, and has only deepened after years of debate and reform. It seems we are no closer to a collective answer than we were when *Ideology, Culture, and the Process of Schooling* was written.

Giroux was correct when he claimed that the possibility for reforming teacher education programs can best be grasped "through an analysis of ways in which power, ideology, biography, and history mediate between schools and the social and economic determinants of the dominant social order" (1981, p. 144). As we have stated above, this claim remains pertinent today, and it gives some indication of why Giroux's theoretical contributions to education and schooling are so significant. Even though the specific claims from given ideological and special-interest groups might vary, the overarching demand for teacher-education programs to reflect the social and economic circumstances of the place and time is powerful.

At the present time the most strident demand is for teacher education programs to reflect the upsurge in technological communication. Giroux points to the vocationalization of colleges of education. This gets lived out in the growing emphasis on technical training of teachers. He claims that this approach to teacher education lacks "any broad sense of vision, meaning, or motivation regarding the role that colleges of education might play in expanding the 'scope of democracy and democratic institutions'" (Giroux & Shannon, 1997, p. 237). It is obvious that teachers need to be able to master and use the information and communication technologies that are available, but these technologies must be seen as tools and not as ends in themselves.

Giroux always reminds us that the questions about teacher education are political in nature because "they serve to define specific roles (teacher, student, principal) through the language they use and the assumptions and the research they consider essential to the teaching profession" (1981, p. 146). Teachers and students must build the answers to these questions and concerns on a foundation of democratic equity that allows for a diversity of worldviews and experiences to be affirmed. Giroux believes that this process can be helped by an emphasis on the place of language and culture. In part, he urges that we use language in a way that stresses the connection between theory and practice. He states, "The language of theory is crucial to the degree that it is grounded in real life experiences, issues, and practices. Theory must begin to address the range of complex issues and events that give meaning to everyday life" (Giroux & Shannon, 1997, p. 240). In faculties and colleges of education we are confronted with demands for the practical. Of course, the practical cannot live without the theoretical. Still, we as teacher educators need to come to grips with this dichotomy. We are quite good at talking about praxis; but it has to be praxis for our students and not merely from our long memory.

"Colleges of education are uniquely suited to developing a language for rethinking the complex dynamics of cultural and material power within an expanded notion of the public, solidarity, and democratic struggle" (Giroux & Shannon, 1997, p. 245). Teacher-education programs need to be above the dictates of particular paradigm groups. Education is simply too important for that. Giroux and Aronowitz contest that neither teacher-training institutions nor the public schools have viewed themselves historically as important sites for educating teachers as intellectuals. They go on to explain that this is true in part because of "the pervasiveness of a growing technocratic rationality that separates theory from practice and contributes to the development of modes of pedagogy that ignore teacher creativity and insight" (1993, p. 41). This technocratic rationality certainly influences how teachers are prepared in universities and colleges. Programs in these institutions insist that prospective teachers master pedagogical techniques that are divorced from crucial questions of purpose, critique, and possibility. That, in part, accounts for the fact that so many teachers can tell you what they did in class, but are less comfortable in discussing why they did it. This is not the fault of teachers. We all have to take responsibility for this fault.

In an earlier writing called "Teacher Education and Social Control," Giroux claimed, "the nature and role of theory in many teacher-education programs provide little or no explanatory power" (Giroux & Purpel, 1983, p. 414). This statement from Giroux's early writing offers valuable insights into his developing thoughts during the following two decades. For us, one of the most disturbing aspects of this quotation is that it could be written for many of today's teacher education programs. Of course, this does not represent the total reality. We suspect that in most universities and colleges that offer teacher-education programs, there are serious pockets of educators who strive to get beyond the technocratic notion of theory and practice. This is certainly true of our own institution.

Many prominent conservatives, Giroux claims, have a contempt for critical thinking and social criticism, and see "the ideal university as an apolitical public sphere inhabited largely by a disinterested faculty engaged in an ahistorical conversation among great minds and pedagogically bound to hand down the ideas and values of the classics to a new generation of would-be thinkers" (1997b, p, 139). In *Fugitive Cultures*, Giroux writes that the prevailing and conservative view of universities is that they "should simply impart knowledge that is outside of the political and cultural whirlwinds of the time" (1996, pp. 120–121). In other words the university should remain detached. Giroux realizes that the university is a major public sphere in so far as it influences massive numbers of people. This is especially true of teacher education faculties, whose teachers go on to influence large numbers of students. It follows that those who are interested in public education must appreciate the link between teacher education and schools. However, Giroux is quite aware that "there is a deep suspicion of any attempt to open up the possibility for educators to address important social problems and to connect them to their teaching" (p. 125). We have to wonder why so many in the halls of dominant society insist that the hard questions not be asked. Giroux would say:

> Higher education represents the possibility of retaining one important democratic public sphere that offers the conditions for resisting the increasing depoliticization of the citizenry, provides a language to challenge the politics of accommodation that connects education to the logic of privatization, refuses to define students as simply consuming subjects, and actively opposes the view of teaching as market-driven practice and learning as a form of training. (Giroux & Myrsiades, 2001, p. 10)

We can't afford to lose that!

We believe that the selection of Giroux's writings that we have framed under *Reading Giroux* allows us to go on to the second part of the book, *Teaching Giroux*. These readings form a minimum core of concepts and topics that will inform our work at the sites we noted at the beginning of the text. We wish to restate that we fully realize that these concepts and topics, as they are presented, cannot be read in isolation. They form their own nexus—to each other, and to larger conceptual webs.

Teaching Giroux

Pedagogy

The major impetus to develop this book comes from the desire of many of our students and colleagues to integrate Giroux's version of critical and reflective pedagogy into the educational processes and into other spheres of peoples' daily lives. We have been able to use Giroux's work, some of which is quoted and referred to throughout this book, in many different ways in our various pedagogical and cultural projects. We realize that we are not alone in doing such work. It is just that we have decided to systematically develop and articulate this Giroux-inspired work.

This second part of *Reading and Teaching Henry Giroux* will contextualize, describe, and share some practical aspects of our pedagogical and cultural projects. The conceptual framework used here is a reader-focused narrative. It is our hope that the material presented in both parts of the book will prove supportive to the actions of many others who are involved in similar pedagogical and cultural projects similar to ours. We present two general sites where we integrate Giroux's work in our practice. These two general sites are presented under the chapter titles of "Pedagogy" and "Teaching Internship". Under "Pedagogy" we present our work in classroom teaching, graduate research, and public pedagogy. In addition to this we offer a reading guide to the Giroux writings we use in our pedagogy. Under "Teaching Internship" we share our work in teacher education, with particular emphasis on the teaching internship program. It is our hope that the readings and the comments on those readings offered in the *Reading Giroux* part of the book enables us to teach students about Giroux's writings more effectively, and to use his work to inform our own efforts. This attempt to organize a selection of Giroux's writings is a systematic response to the interest in, and value of, his work. The voices of our students, colleagues, and cultural workers are an essential part of this work.

Classroom Teaching

Autobiographical Sketches

In an attempt to introduce Henry Giroux's work to our students, we begin by asking them to get to know something about the person by reading his autobiographical comments, his biographical sketches, and various interviews done with him. Next we discuss the form of language that Giroux uses in his writings. Students are asked to read Giroux's writings in which he explains his use of a particular form of language. He calls it a language of critique, hope, and possibility. Finally, students are asked to read his writings on his own teaching style. We will discuss why we follow this sequence, how it enables us to introduce Giroux's major concepts to students, and how students empower themselves to engage his work. In our experience, this sequence enables us all to engage Giroux's writings in a more meaningful way.

Beginning the first class in a new semester is not an easy task for us, even after many years of teaching experience. Like many other university teachers, we have to gather our thoughts and decide how we are going to approach this new group of students. How are we going to introduce the content and structure of the course? How are we going to invite students to participate in class discussions and various other activities? How do we encourage them to invest their time and energy in this particular course? How are we going to see if it will be a positive experience for them? If we were only interested in transmission, we could simply point them to the appropriate web site. But pedagogy must involve more than that.

Over the years, we have tried different approaches in teaching Giroux's material. We have found it productive to give some overview comments on his work and the work of other writers we use, and to touch upon some of the key issues. In other words, we put Giroux's work in context. We also try to put our introductory comments into the macro contexts of the issues with which we are dealing. We have found that student responses vary to our approaches. "It seemed like a lot of issues to be trying to get across right away. Probably as we get more into this section of the course there will be greater interaction and contributions" (George).

We have learned to capitalize on students' curiosity about Giroux's background and his work. These are some of the questions we hear. Who is this person? What is his background? Where is he from? What makes him write the way he does? Whose ideas does he problematize? Who are the other writers that engage in similar issues? How do Giroux's writings compare with other writers? Are people outside North America interested in similar issues? What are they saying about the issues Giroux presents? Why does Giroux use a particular form of language when he writes? Why doesn't he communicate in a simple and clear language? What do others think about his writings? Why has he become such a significant intellectual figure in North America and in other parts of the world? Why should one bother to read his writings? How does Giroux make his living? What relationship does he have with his family? How does he teach? What does he want to achieve personally? What does he expect others to achieve?

This book, among other things, is an attempt to help answer these questions. In our initial classes, we add comments on Giroux's background by directing students' attention to Giroux's writings in which he discloses his background. To help us deal with these questions we depend on Giroux's autobiographical sketches, which are scattered through many of his writings. Primarily we use *Border Crossings*; *Between Borders*; *Channel Surfing*; *Fugitive Cultures*; and *Disturbing Pleasures*. We also use the comments made by other writers about Giroux's work. Therefore, in this section of the book we make use of biographical sketches, as well as the interviews that he has given. We have observed that students like to read this material and feel at ease with his description of how he grew up and what he did over a period of time. This material helps students identify with Giroux in a more sympathetic fashion. They feel that Giroux is explaining to them the tensions and contradictions of school life, and showing them what possibilities exist for struggle within the everyday functioning of their schools. Students' confidence seems to grow as they ask questions and engage in dialogue about Giroux.

Another way that Giroux's autobiographical sketches develop courage among students and teachers is by developing some degree of understanding about how he deals with the micropolitics of everyday work life. Where does he get the courage to challenge administration and colleagues? How does he manage to keep his job? How does he manage to keep friends? How does he keep his status in the academic community intact? How does his critical stand on popular culture, schools, society, and culture influence us? The simple fact is that students, colleagues, and their children do watch television, for many hours. Parents do buy Disney toys for their children. They spend lots of money to buy the paraphernalia associated with sports. And not the least, they do take their children to eat at McDonald's and collect the toys that come with eating there. Parents, children and their friends enjoy doing these things. Students and teachers like to know what Giroux does in his daily life and how he interacts with people who enjoy this sort of lifestyle. This conversation is often tempered by our own personal knowledge of Henry Giroux.

Fortunately, Giroux has touched upon the topics above in his autobiographical sketches. The disclosure by Giroux about aspects of his professional and personal life builds trust between him and the students who are reading his writings. When students read about how much he loves his children, how he cares for his friends, and how he respects the work of others, they get a sense of his life at the microlevel. When students read his autobiographical sketches, they realize that it has not always been easy for Giroux. Stanley Aronowitz explains that Giroux is one of "the most publicized of outstanding scholars and intellectuals who suffered from the vindictiveness of the established academic generation that felt threatened by their innovative work" (1993, p. 56). This reality for Giroux has most recently been shown again with his departure from Penn State (An Educator's Reflections on the Crisis in Education and Democracy in the US: An Interview with Henry A. Giroux, Michael Alexander Pozo, www.dissidentvoice.org, September 25, 2004). Students admire him for taking a stand and sticking to his principles, risking, and finally losing his job. They appreciate the way he handled his encounter with the President of Boston University, and they realize that Giroux fully understood, at that moment in John Silber's office, that his academic freedom was being assaulted. They see for themselves that Giroux is capable of courage. This is especially true when Giroux talks about his experience at Boston University and explains the political and ideological views of the university president (1997b). As a young assistant professor, he could have taken the Silber offer, and melted into Boston University. This was his crucible. Giroux's response was an example of lived courage in the face of an entrenched ideological force. This act alone enables students and teachers to understand what Giroux means, when he says students and teachers should engage in practices that help them to develop civic courage. Giroux urges teachers and students to become transformative intellectuals, and cultural workers. He wants them to become public intellectuals. He urges teachers, students, and other cultural workers, as public intellectuals to do transformative work in the public spheres. By public spheres Giroux means other places, often outside of school, where teachers and students gather, interact, and live their daily lives. These places are communities, churches, clubs, meeting halls, cafeterias, pubs, and the like.

What students appreciate most in Giroux's writings is that he seems sensitive to their voices and locations. They do not feel he is patronizing them. This is perhaps because students can identify with Giroux's description of his own school life, how he: played basketball, hung around the street corner, listened to music, lived, and enjoyed his working-class culture. Building on these kinds of attitudes among students, we find spaces to infuse our own intentions into classroom interaction with them. We try to be open about our intentions and agendas; of course, we fully appreciate that students have other agendas. That is not a problem. Our intention in this particular instance is to encourage students to read and understand Giroux's writings. For example, when students are deriving pleasure from reading about Giroux's youthful street-corner lifestyle, we tell them that he did manage to see beyond the limits that his particular working-class culture imposed on him. He did manage to attend college and succeed in getting his doctoral degree. Not only that, he did manage to become a leading intellectual figure in North America and elsewhere. At this point, we find it easier to introduce Giroux's notion of pedagogy of hope to our students. We find, as does Giroux, that in the context of current dominant conservative educational and economic reforms, students are overburdened by discourses of despair. This is true for graduate and undergraduate students. As youth they are often devalued. They are sometimes told that they are lazy, underachievers, and underproductive (2003a). They are told that they lack needed skills and knowledge, and therefore are unfit to participate in a neoliberal global economy. If the graduate students we are talking to are practicing teachers, then most of the woes of modern society are seen as their fault.

Similarly, at this point, we draw students' attention to Giroux's critical writings on popular culture—his writings about television, movies, radio, fashion, and video, and the like. We find that students generally are impressed by Giroux's ability to provide critical theoretical categories to analyze popular culture. This is particularly true of his analysis of various movies, fashion, advertisements and other aspects of the popular culture. However, students do not always agree with his interpretations and come up with their own analysis. This allows us, as educators, to build on Giroux's insistence on the significance of students' voices in the context of classroom learning and teaching. We believe we need to ask many more questions about popular culture if we are to make it part of our pedagogy. For example, we need to ask the following questions: What relationship is there between classroom work and students' lives outside the class? Is it possible to incorporate aspects of students' culture into schoolwork in a fashion that goes beyond merely confirming what they already know? Can we incorporate students' culture without trivializing it? We believe we need to keep these questions before us as we teach. We draw students' attention to Giroux's writings where he explains how "language is inseparable from lived experience and from how people create a distinctive voice" (1997a, p. 121). We encourage students to come up with their own language of critique about movies, fashion, and advertisements. When they do this and they feel empowered.

Once this form of identification has been achieved, we invite students to reflect on their own experiences. We create a safe space and time for them to voice their own backgrounds and experiences. We invite students to anticipate the unfolding of their own lifespan, as well as voice their hopes and concerns. We go beyond hearing and listen to them carefully and recognize and affirm the authenticity of their voices. We realize that to hear and to listen can be two very different approaches to creating safe spaces. It must be stated that we take students very seriously. We appreciate that they have varied and complex lives. We are aware that many of the students who attend our university have to hold down a number of part-time jobs in order to pay tuition and survive. We are acutely aware that there are very active food banks on our campus. We applaud those students who are under stress, who are young single parents, who cope with difficult personal relationships, and who still manage to educate themselves. Everyday, they defy all odds. Therefore what pedagogical work we do with them, is done gently while holding high expectations for their contribution to the process.

While doing this, we are sensitive to those safe spaces we have tried to open for our students. We are ready to infuse our teacher authority if students linger too long in using the language of despair while anticipating the future. It is not uncommon in the present sociopolitical-cultural-economic context for students to take up the language of despair. Students are constantly told about the declining value of schooling and intellectual life, and about the hardship associated with not finding good jobs after they graduate from university. If despair begins to overshadow the classroom setting, we practice and encourage the language of hope. While respecting their present reality, we suggest that it is possible to imagine, and then carve out, a lifestyle that could sustain them. We point out to our students that possibilities exist for them to empower themselves. There are multiple lifestyles that one could imagine, create, and enjoy. This is one of the important things to keep in mind. We stress to students that they can, within reason, create or reconstruct themselves. This is the essence of hope. This, for us, is teaching Giroux. We have given ourselves the power to shift the curriculum beyond transmission by using it as a base to interrogate local and global circumstances. We try to do this with our students. We also have to be willing to adjust the curriculum we may have developed a semester earlier, to accommodate students whose experiences and interests do not replicate the students we worked with at an earlier time. If we hope to nudge students on to critical thought and action, we have to operate this way.

At this juncture, students are often interested in our own life stories as teachers. They usually like to know how growing up was for us. How did we end up having the lifestyle of a university professor? This gives us an opening to disclose our own experiences, attitudes, and feelings to students. Very often this revelation is done over time. The sentiments and comfort levels of the students have to be kept in mind. More often than not, this exercise creates a warm classroom atmosphere conducive to teaching and learning. It often dissolves unnecessary authority barriers that usually exist in the beginning of the class between the teacher and students.

On the other hand, there are occasions where students are shy or overwhelmed with our authority as university teachers. We have to acknowledge that many of the students we work with are postdegree, and have had four years of academic conditioning. Given this reality, students often hesitate to openly ask us about our own personal lives. Practicing reflection-in-action, at the appropriate moment, we take the initiative to open up spaces for ourselves in which we inject biographical sketches of our own. Very often these spaces are linked to course content. We have found that students take an interest in knowing about us as their teachers.

When we teach undergraduate or graduate students, we often tell them that we have had a wide range of educational experience. This sharing is most self-serving, in so far as students and teachers put great value on experience. One of our colleagues talks about "the tyranny of experience," and we have come to give greater value to this dictum. This is especially true when we try to balance experience with theory, as it applies to teaching. Of course, students have their own views of the whole disclosure process. "I like it when professors share a little of themselves to their students. It shows us that you are human like everyone else. We are starting to realize that Professors have deadlines and lives of their own" (Mary).

One of the challenges we face in teaching our students is how to get them involved in making sense of the changing world around us. How do we communicate to them the complex relationship between school and society; education and the larger social and cultural changes that are taking place? The challenge is also to give our students the conceptual tools to see the changing world critically and reflectively. We have found Henry Giroux's work helps us greatly in this matter.

Biographical Sketches

A number of the people who have collaborated with Giroux have provided biographical information about his professional and personal development. In relation to the biographical sketches we use with our students, we read Aronowitz in *Ideology Culture and the Process of Schooling*; McLaren in *Teachers as Intellectuals*; Kincheloe, McLaren, and Steinberg in *Pedagogy and the Politics of Hope*; and McLaren and Freire in *Teachers as Intellectuals*. Teachers and students find these biographical sketches very useful in understanding Giroux's writings. The commentaries on Giroux's work and background, by Aronowitz, McLaren, Freire, Kincheloe, Steinberg and others, are extremely useful in introducing Giroux's work to undergraduate and graduate students. We also find this material to be useful in teacher in-service and teaching internship programs. This work enables students and others to identify with Giroux and sympathetically understand him as a person and as a leading theorist in the area of critical and reflective education and pedagogy. Much of the biographical material we are referring to here has been presented in the *Reading Giroux* part of the book.

Interviews

Students often ask questions about critical theory, radical education, struggle and the like. Many of these concepts are never easy, for any of us. In this regard we find Giroux's interviews indispensable. We have found that the two interviews in *Border Crossings* and the one in *Disturbing Pleasures* to be most helpful. We find that the interviews readily available on the World Wide Web are also helpful. We ask students to read them following our introductory discussion. We find that reading Giroux's interviews and listening to them on the web serve as an opening for us to discuss many topics, issues, and concerns. Another factor that we like about the interviews is that we can see passion and the hope in them. Many of the thoughts, concepts, and suggestions that Giroux offers through his interviews are found in the *Reading Giroux* part of this book.

Language

We believe that Giroux is one of the most prolific writers who has accepted the challenge of teaching students critically and reflectively. His writings are complex: sometimes undergraduates find his work difficult to understand. "I believe the ideas in these articles could be expressed in simpler language, so more people could get more out of them" (Hannah). In this situation, we try to encourage the students not to give up after the initial attempt at reading this new material. "You seemed to suggest that we not be limited or 'put off' by the complexity of the book. You suggested that we have to look beyond these complexities to draw conclusions that we can apply in a variety of ways" (Joe). Giroux himself is acutely aware of the criticism about the difficulty of language. As indicated above, our students raise questions about his use of language. We attempt to explain to them the various issues involved in the use of language. Fortunately, Giroux has responded to his critics who object to his particular use of language. He claims that the struggle over language often is concerned with clarity, complexity, and the redefinition of terms. Giroux believes that such a position is too reductionist. "When people say that we write in a language that isn't as clear as it could be, while that might be true they're also responding to the unfamiliarity of a paradigm that generates questions suppressed in the dominant culture" (1993, p. 150). He also reminds us that there is no universal standard of language that becomes a referent for all others. We have learned over the years that the effort is worth it. We also believe that Giroux offers great insight in relating education to a changing society. His cultural writings are most helpful in making sense of changes that are taking place around us.

Teaching

Giroux's agenda is clear. He states that his overriding pedagogical project was rooted "in an attempt at majority democratic education, that is, an education whose aim was to advance the ideological and lived relations necessary for students at least to interrogate the possibility of addressing schooling as a site of ongoing struggle" (1997a, 171).

As teachers, and teacher educators, we also look to examine Giroux's style of teaching. Our students, and the teachers we work with, also show an interest in knowing how Giroux teaches his students. Students find it interesting reading Giroux's description of his own teaching style. He writes that in the past he organized his courses around selected critical texts where he combined introductory lectures with a seminar format "in which students were asked to engage the texts actively by reading them oppositionally. Though this approach attempted to make the class more democratic, it failed to unsettle the kinds of social relations that characterize teacher-centered environments" (1997a, p. 170). Giroux thinks that there are many reasons for such a result. First of all he believes that the language of theory intimidates students. Students claim that the assigned texts were too difficult to read and that they simply could not make the connection between the readings and any practical application to education. In many ways, students felt that they were being asked to read and speak in a language that was foreign to them. Giroux realized that "many students have not problematized the ways in which traditional schooling has shaped their perceptions of power, learning, and identity" (p. 170). He explains that many of his students simply did not believe that their voices counted. They believed that their role, as students, was to receive. Another thing that Giroux realized about his classes was that "whenever class discussion did occur it was more often than not dominated by males, especially white males, in spite of the fact that women often constituted over 50% of my classes" (p. 170). Giroux also found it disconcerting that students set him up as an authority figure. It became clear to Giroux that despite his use of oppositional material and seminar format, he was reproducing a pedagogical relationship that did not provide students "with the opportunity to speak in a safe space and to appropriate power in the class in order to deconstruct the texts and engage in collective self-criticism and a critique of the politics of [his] location as a teacher" (p. 171). We can readily see how this reality would be troublesome for Giroux. We often find ourselves in similar situations. It should be added that this situation often varies according to the academic experiences of students. We find that graduate students have a much stronger sense of place and voice. This is to be expected. Many of them have been able to penetrate the transmission model that was part and parcel of their undergraduate studies.

In time, Giroux attempted to address some of these concerns. It should be added that for many university teachers this would not be a problem. Giroux was willing to experiment with his pedagogical practices by organizing his courses around particular writing assignments. Part of the agenda here was to create a "third space" in the classroom. In our own work we talk about creating "safe spaces." Of course we are interested in contrasting the concept of third space with our own use of safe space.

Giroux cautions us to be aware of pedagogical practices that distance students from their histories and lived experiences. He believes that it is crucial to give students more control over the conditions of their own knowledge production. Giroux writes about reproducing "the binarism of being politically enlightened in [his] theorizing and pedagogically wrong in [his] organization of concrete class relations" (1997a, p. 171). His answer was to use, what he called "border writing." This border writing was meant to be defined less as a technical exercise "in skill development than as a form of cultural production that more closely articulated the relationship between my political project as a progressive teacher and the underlying principles and practices that informed the organization and character of my class" (p. 171). He linked the use of writing assignments to encouraging students to theorize their own experiences. This was done, in part, by having his students examine how representations signify and position them through the institutional and ideological authority such representations carry in the dominant culture. Giroux, of course, had other goals for his course work. We are pointing out aspects of those pedagogical practices that impact on our own work with students.

Giroux was brave, we believe, to introduce the course by talking about power in the classroom. Very often students and teachers walk into the classroom knowing what the power relationships are, and then spend so much energy and time making certain that those relationships are maintained. Giroux does not back away from teacher authority. "I also made clear the rationale for the authority I exercised in the course and how that authority was intended to be used to expand rather than restrict the possibility for student agency" (1997a, p. 172). Giroux was also honest enough to relinquish all claims to objectivity. He also attempted to refute, before his students, the usual claim "that teachers were disinterested, that knowledge was unproblematic, and that teaching was merely a methodology for transmitting information" (p. 172). We have found that our students are impressed by Giroux's courage in disclosing his teaching style publicly.

Students and teachers often voice their concerns about writing down their own teaching styles. "The workload is rather heavy and we all feel that the quality of the work will suffer as a result of rushing through it. Hopefully, this will be taken into account when we are evaluated" (Sam). This is not an uncommon response or request. We all find it easier to evaluate or comment on the teaching styles of others. We find, for example, in our own work with teaching interns that it is much easier for them to reflect on their cooperating teachers' teaching styles than publicly acknowledge the shortcomings in their styles. Of course, it is easier for us to reflect on our own teaching privately. Generally most of us find it difficult to make those reflections public. Sometimes this adds tension in our classroom discussions, yet we believe that learning to be reflective is crucial. Therefore we proceed with caution.

Major Concepts

As part of our process in using Giroux's writings in our classes, we like to provide students with articles that give them a comprehensive look at the major concepts of critical theory and pedagogy as developed by authors such as Kanpol, McLaren, Aronowitz, Freire, Wink, and others. Students are open to such discussion. "Critical thinking and theorizing are very important fundamentals of education. However, this type of discussion should occur at a time in the term when students are not under pressure to complete so many assignment projects" (Tim).

Expanding the Discussion

Earlier, we explained the reasons for using Giroux's writings. For example, we have explained why we find it more suitable to start with Giroux's autobiographical and biographical sketches. In addition to these readings we have identified several concepts Giroux uses when he writes an article, chapter, or book. For example, let us consider Giroux's *Teacher Education as Cultural Politics* (2005b, p. 188). In this writing, he talks about power, language, history, culture, student experience, student voice, the public sphere, and a critical pedagogy for the classroom. When we ask our students to read this particular piece by Giroux, we draw their attention to the various concepts Giroux uses to develop his arguments. We ask students what they know about these concepts? Some students take up this challenge, and articulate these concepts and relationships among themselves, and then come up with their own narratives about schooling, society, and education. For example, on the topic of diversity one of our students wrote: "I find it ironic if you talk to young children of different cultures, they will have little problem getting along. Something changes as they get older and this is culture. We need to get back to this childhood innocence" (Jemma). In relation to change, one student had this to say: "If we resist change and decide to let others govern our thoughts, feelings, and opinions, then we only regress and lose our freedom of speech" (Chester). Democracy is always a very crucial discussion for students. "It seems as though the development of democracy has always involved someone or some group having all the power over the majority of citizens. Is this a true democracy or a hidden form of dictatorship" (Gord).

Many of our university students are willing to examine their own academic backgrounds. "I feel that science and technology are a very critical part to a child's education. However, it is not the most important aspect. Teaching children to be integral parts of society holds this position" (Jeb). Naturally, gender was a very tumultuous topic. "I particularly enjoyed the two views on women's rights, one from a male perspective and one from a female. It was interesting to see how serious most females take this issue, and males take it much less seriously" (Dan). Language is always a very vital topic. "I can really see the relationship between what we're saying about language and its power to free or to enslave. Using your example of South Africa I can see how using language like this can create justification for an unjust state of affairs" (Rose). The concept of the other is an intriguing one for our students. "This was a valuable exercise. I am interested in this whole notion of otherness, the other. I'm not sure, as social animals, we can define ourselves without appeal to another—whether person, group, gender, race, etc." (Sarah). The topic of race brings many worldviews to the front. "I think people are too concerned with racial issues. This is causing a great deal of tension to build in society" (Jim).

Naturally, this type of teaching is often a source of comment and resistance. "This [undergraduate] course is shaping up to be much different from the others. The emphasis on theories is an interesting diversion from the practical, focused, 'teaching-oriented' content of other courses" (Lora). Students are usually quite vocal on other topics such as advertisements, movies, abuse, reform, youth, relationships, video, music, art, future, and work. We then ask them what the source of their information is. In other words, we encourage them to reflect on why they talk about these concepts the way they do. What are some other ways to talk about them? How do sociologists, psychologists, economists, and others talk about these concepts? Then, we ask them to read Giroux's article critically. In other words, we expect students to problematize Giroux's writings.

As university teachers we are interested in introducing Giroux's perspectives on varied concepts to our students. However, we do not want to simply transmit Giroux's ideas to our students. Our purpose is to encourage students to engage Giroux's work critically. We draw their attention to three forms of knowledge: the common sense knowledge, the professional knowledge, and the state knowledge. We explained that the common sense knowledge is based mainly on one's own subjective experiences, rooted in one's own language, family, community, region, country, gender, race and class. Those who are trained in academic areas such as political science, anthropology, history, philosophy and other disciplines generally produce professional knowledge. Various organs of the government such as the Department of Health, the Department of Education, and the like produce state knowledge. We encourage our students to be aware of the forms of knowledge they are using during their conversations with others, especially in the classroom situation. We urge them to combine these three forms of knowledge in their conversations, analysis, and writings on issues relating to school, society, and education. We find that in this way we are usually able to integrate Giroux's writings in our teaching effectively. This does not mean that all our students become critical thinkers. "I have found the reading very interesting and the readings that I have been able to really study have had an impact on the way I think. I am at a stage now where I cannot absorb or reflect on the material. I am merely attempting to get through it" (Paula). We pass Giroux's reminder on to students that teaching is complex, "much more complex than mastering a body of knowledge and implementing curriculums. The thing about teaching is that the specificity of the context is always central. We can't get away with invoking rules and procedures that cut across contexts" (1993, p. 17).

Teachers' work is even more complicated because it can't guarantee any qualitative change in a short period of time. Giroux is again helpful here when he admits that students might not change their minds from having been in his class. He fully realizes that students have to make up their own minds and that "the most we can do as educators is to provide teachers [and students] with a sense of what it means to limit their role to being technicians or to take up what it means to be a public intellectual" (1994, p. 170).

In his writings, Giroux emphasizes that teachers, and those students who want to be teachers, should function as public intellectuals. They should not be trained merely to play the role of technicians. However, he provides us with an interesting insight when he claims that most students are content with seeing themselves as technicians and clerks. Our students have their own understanding of that dilemma. "We may be thinking about the practical aspects of teaching more so than the abstract and theoretical. A lot of our minds seem to rebel against these discourses at a time when we have other things to consider" (Ruby). Giroux realizes, and our experience bears it out, that for students to be suddenly exposed to a line of critical thinking is not always comfortable for them. In the type of reflective and critical classes we hold, students often are asked to examine their own attitudes, value systems, and practices. This is particularly upsetting for some experienced teachers who feel that their teaching is being brought into question. Of course, part of the problem is that students do not always have "a frame of reference or a vocabulary with which to articulate the centrality of what they do. They are caught up in market logic and bureaucratic jargon" (Giroux, 1993, p. 16). It might seem that Giroux is highlighting the deficiency inherent in students' ability to understand complex issues which critical pedagogy attempts to engage. He is not interested in any deficient model, we believe. Instead, he is very much interested in students' backgrounds and experiences.

In our own teaching, we find that students are worried about learning skills, techniques, and forms of knowledge that would get them jobs in the current economic, political, and social climate. "When I finished my B.A. I was happy and proud. Yet my older family members continuously asked me, 'But what can you do with it?' I hope I have a great job some day soon but I don't necessarily associate education with utility" (Claire). The concerns of many parents seem to be the same.

It comes as no surprise to us when our students shy away from discussing the meaning of radical democracy. Their first reaction is that the notion of democracy is too abstract. Generally, we find that many students feel uncomfortable when they are asked to engage in discussions on inequalities—social, political, cultural, economic, and psychological. Some groups of students find it difficult to discuss issues of race, class, and gender. In our teaching, we need to take students' sensitivities about these issues into account. Students have their own experiences about inequalities, race, and gender. "There will always be discrimination about class, race, education, sex, and physical appearance. If minorities can get a real say into their children's education then the discrimination and the inferiority complex can be reduced" (Darren). In the process of free voice, and open dialectic, we have to allow all claims. "Political and religious freedom, women's rights, racism, oppression are all topics which are not ever going to end. People have their own views and will not change them" (Herb). Giroux is very willing to allow expressions of such realities. "Students have memories, families, religion, feelings, languages, and cultures that give them a distinctive voice. We can critically engage that experience and we can move beyond it. But we can't deny it" (1993, p. 17). One of Giroux's main points is that learning has to be meaningful to students before it can become critical. He realizes that our problem is that we have a theory of knowledge but no real theory of pedagogy.

In addition to students' experiences and backgrounds, there are many institutional difficulties in integrating Giroux's version of critical pedagogy. Many institutions of higher education have implemented "restructuring." This has become a magic word in the educational reform movement of the last two decades. Giroux has critically evaluated the meaning of structural changes brought about by this reform movement at various levels of educational institutions, including higher education, and faculties or schools of education. These changes have an impact on our teaching and on our functioning as intellectuals and cultural workers.

During significant changes at our faculty teacher-education programs have been redesigned. This has often meant the shortening of programs and the elimination of full courses in many areas, sometimes to the consternation of students. "I feel that this course has too much material to cover in a six-week time frame. I think the workload is too much" (Sharon). The courses referred to here have been divided into units. This of necessity has resulted in the shortening or condensation of course material in an attempt to integrate various disciplines. Research and critical discussions pertaining to multiculturalism, race, gender, class, democracy, citizenship, public spheres, and the like have to be spread over various courses. Only a limited amount of time is available to discuss these issues. This is the space where competing ideologies, goals and purposes of education, philosophies of education, social theories, and theories of pedagogies interact. Conservative, liberal, radical, feminist, critical, and other discourses surface with varying degrees and intensities during the decision-making process regarding what should be included in the course. Of course, our students have their own agendas. "Perhaps you could relate categorical statements to contemporary issues or provide us with some statistics, for example, of the purported astronomical profits which some corporations are making in an era of budget slashing and increasing cutbacks" (Seb). There are further questions concerning how the course should be taught and evaluated and by whom. Needless to say, macropolitics at the institutional level is intensified during this time. Students, teachers, administrators, professors and other stakeholders in education, such as businesses, unions, government, consultants and specialists of all sorts, participate in the social construction of the curriculum process, and the delivery of the curriculum in the classroom. Such participation is always contaminated by the perception they hold about their locations in the institutional structure. Self-interest is often given priority, that is, it becomes an overriding concern. Questions regarding tenure, promotion, workload, rewards or lack of them, status, prestige, and power become paramount. People generally worry about their families and their future. So in this context, "living dangerously" is difficult to practice. To practice "border crossing," while "living in exile" or being "homeless", and functioning as a "cultural worker" can indeed be hard for many people. This is not to say that people are totally incapable of acting in these ways. People do transform their actions, behaviors, and lives, but they do so slowly and cautiously. Many people do come to see themselves, and act as, intellectuals in the moderate sense of the term. Our students are aware of such possibilities. "I think we should try to feminize science. In order to fix the problem, I think males in early school years should be educated that we are all equal. Young girls should be encouraged to engage in any field they wish" (Louise).

Giroux's pedagogical writings, on the notions of language of hope and despair, have proven to be extremely useful for us as we interact with people in the particular institutional setting where we work. We found his insights on these two notions enabling during the period of restructuring. In fact, reading Giroux helped us map the process more critically. We have been able to take advantage of many new spaces opened by the restructuring process of Faculty. As we will explain in the next section, we have been able to build a reflective and critical teaching internship and teaching program amidst these institutional changes.

Similarly, in the classroom situation, we have been able to integrate critical and reflective components in our course contents to a reasonable degree. As might be expected, the big constraint is the one of class time and the number of students with whom we have to work. "The issues that were raised in class are very good. We may have done the written work if this part was 12 weeks but I know we will not get everything done" (Cindy). Yet, it has been possible for us to spend a reasonable time introducing Giroux's version of critical pedagogy to our students. We have been able to teach freely within the mode of reflective and critical pedagogy. Our interest in teaching Giroux's work to our students as well as our experience working within this particular educational setting offered a real impetus to produce this book.

One of the vital discussions we had in class had to do with the various critical texts we use. "Today's class caused me to realize something that I have known all the while, that people control what we read and learn. Teachers make matters worse by assigning specific texts and other literature to read" (Norman). Another issue that usually comes up in teaching Giroux's work to our students is that we have to Canadianize it. Our students invariably voice their concern that his books are "too American" and that they find it difficult to relate to the examples presented in them. Giroux talks about educational reforms in the United States, and often provides analysis of the reform in terms of ongoing debates among conservatives, liberals, and radicals in the context of the Regan/Bush/Bush eras. In his work he discusses cultural wars going on in the United States. In many of his books he talks about race issues in the context of Los Angeles riots or 9/11. Similarly, his work is full of the history of education at all levels in the United States. That is his context, and we have to respect that. Many students in Canada find it difficult to relate to the discussion embedded in the context of the United States politics, educational history, and the history of race in large urban centers. "It has caused me to pay close attention to the background of authors, including nationality, ethnicity, religion, and educational background before using a particular source" (Adam). We have to find ways around this working problem. We have to work these borders. We know that Giroux from his long-term work in Canada is very aware of the issues with which we deal. We also appreciate the writings of Canadian scholars who are truly border crossers in the most helpful sense of the phrase.

However, when it comes to Giroux's analysis of Hollywood films, fashion industry and sports, then our students relate to his work with great enthusiasm. They find themselves getting engaged in his analyses, although they do not always agree with his interpretations. The same is true with Giroux's work on video and music. Students find it quite interesting and valuable. "It was very interesting to note how the media and corporations use images and their own perceptions of what they consider to be acceptable to maintain the status quo. They often do not portray the reality of these things" (Wade). Of course, the world is open to many interpretations. "I do realize the advertising element in movies and all the marketing schemes behind them. You should be critical of movies and advertising, but I think that sometimes you can over-analyze things" (Janet). On the other hand, Giroux's writings on violence and crime in the urban centers of the United States are difficult to relate to, and our students tell us that. Of course, it is our hope that they will never have to relate to that in the same way. In the beginning, when our students voiced their concerns the way they did, we felt a little bit surprised. We thought that most Canadian students would be familiar with these issues in the United States, owing to the fact that American television shows and newscasts have been dominating the Canadian scene for a long time. To our surprise again, many of the students do not watch the news—Canadian or American. They watch other shows selectively. In other words, the students are not always the passive audience we make them out to be.

We find three strategies work well in these classroom-teaching situations. The first strategy we take is to ask the students what they know about who produces textbooks, movies, educational videos, and other related material in North America. Where does the financial power lie in these areas? How big, in terms of dollars, are these industries? Who has control over distribution and consumption of educational material? Who writes curriculum material for whom? Together with our students we raise many other such questions. Students' responses vary. Some students seem to know a lot about these questions and have access to the language of the political economy of production, distribution and the consumption of educational material. Some students know about how multinational corporations function, and therefore, have access to that set of language or discourses. Often these students have taken some sociology, political science, or history courses. In this way, students realize that many of the big publishing houses reside in the United States and therefore most books are American.

As a second strategy, we attempt to encourage students to discuss these issues in historical and comparative contexts. We try to raise the level of discussion by infusing "mini lectures" on the development of the British Empire in North America and explain to our students how the United States and Canada were once British colonies. We talk about the development of capitalism as a global force. We discuss how the great colonial powers, like England, played an important role in the development of industrial or early capitalism. We touch upon various discourses on imperialism, when and where it warrants infusing this type of knowledge. Most students have heard about the globalization—politically, socially, culturally, and economically—of all aspects of modern life. So, this gives us an opening to infuse critical discussions on globalization, Fordism, post-Fordism, late capitalism, neoliberalism, flexible accumulation, postmodernism, poststructuralism, postcolonial writings and cultural studies. In addition to this we include the voices of aboriginal groups. The goal here is to encourage students to read and discuss this material in a comparative and historical perspective. It will be no surprise to readers to hear that students often hesitate at the amount of reading that we suggest to them. Very often their resistance is most sincere. "I feel that the material in this course is very relevant and allows us to think critically and enter a classroom with an open mind about society and education" (Jay).

To further deepen the discussion of why professors in Canada, by choice or default, use American textbooks we find it useful, as a third strategy, to discuss with students the nationalist and the continentalist perspectives on Canada. Briefly stated, nationalists have generally lamented the domination of Canada by the United States and would like to reduce this dominance in all aspects of Canadian life—economics, political, social and cultural. The fact is that many Canadian institutions are highly integrated with institutions of the United States. On the other hand, continentalists have traditionally viewed the development of North America as a unified process. These short discourses give us as teachers an opportunity to integrate most recent developments affecting North America as a whole. For example, the ongoing discourses of Canadian nationalists and continentalists provide the context in which we can extend these discourses to the discussions of NAFTA and other agreements between the United States, Canada, and Mexico. Building on discussions of NAFTA, we talk about the impact on Canadian education, job training, and human resource development in general. In such discussions we are able to talk about crossing borders in both a literal and a figurative sense. To be sure, we are not claiming that we do all these things, all the time, in all our classes. The purpose of describing the three strategies above is to indicate how teachers and students can contextualize the American material in Canada. The process of contextualizing allows students and teachers to bring Canadian material and read it along side of Giroux's critical writings.

We will discuss one more situation that arises when we attempt to integrate Giroux's writings on race, democracy, gender, and multiculturalism. In his writing on these subjects, Giroux emphasizes that we should respect others in terms of their differences and self-identities. For him, real democracy means reducing inequalities that separate the marginalized people from the mainstream. It also means creating conditions in which justice and fairness becomes the norm, thus improving the life chances of people who have been traditionally denied the opportunity to participate in the opportunity structure of a society. Giroux says that schools should be considered public spheres, where students should learn how to create conditions for democracy. Students should be taught to become good citizens who will have the knowledge to understand how political, economic, and social institutions function in a democratic society. Moreover, such citizens should have the courage to participate in civic culture in order to make their communities and society more equal, just, and fair. However, according to Giroux, although schools could play a necessary role as a site in transforming society based on the principles of radical democracy, they do not always provide sufficient conditions for the development of a radical democracy. For a radical democracy to develop, we need to expand the notion of public spheres. Public spheres can be seen as spaces where citizens debate on various issues effecting their daily lives, independent of the state and economic institutions. These public spheres are not places where citizens involve themselves in the buying and selling of goods and services as they do in the market place. These public spheres are spaces where citizens build relationships and communities and contemplate how they want to live and enjoy their lives. Examples of some of these public spheres are neighborhood clubs, townhouses, church groups, community halls, local sports arenas, theatre groups, and so on.

We indicated earlier that we have observed time and again that some students feel uneasy when they engage in discussions dealing with democracy as outlined by Giroux in his writings. Many students do not believe that inequalities can be completely eliminated in any society. Some students do in fact believe there will always be rich and poor, advantaged and disadvantaged, powerful and less powerful people, no matter what is done, according to some students. These feelings exist both in homogeneous mainstream classrooms in the United States and Canada, and in multicultural classrooms in both countries. Students in both settings want to compete with each other and want to experience individual success rather than worry about the success of the whole group with which they identify themselves. For example, in a multicultural classroom some students do not hesitate to voice concern about how their groups have been discriminated against and marginalized by mainstream institutions and social policies. But this does not mean that they want to get rid of the social stratification within their own groups. They want to be in a privileged position within their own groups; they do not wish to be associated with the under class and less-privileged members of their group. At this level, their aspiration, desire, and ambition is to be associated with the privileged people in all cultural groups, especially with the successful members of the mainstream society. The structure of the classroom in a university setting reinforces these feelings in the sense that students have to be evaluated and graded at the end of the term. There are often attempts by some administrators occupying important positions in the university structure to pressure professors to grade students using the criterion of the bell curve. They usually claim to do this in the name of standards and excellence. This logic escapes us. Giroux, in his writings, has critically analyzed this move on the part of the administration in institutions of higher education, as well as in the public school systems. But the situation we have often faced in our classrooms is that some students want to be graded on the basis of the bell-curve criterion. These students are often relatively more outspoken and in many cases dominate policy making of student unions and organizations. It also has to be noted that these students often have profited from courses and programs that have used some form of bell-curve criterion. It is further true that many students do not want us to mess with the transmission forms of teaching and learning in which they have succeeded. Hegemony rules.

In these situations the best we have been able to do is to admit that total eradication of inequalities in any modern society remains a remote possibility. "We have to recognize there are gender differences and biases within the school as well as outside the school. However, I didn't experience any problems with gender differences or bias, at least I don't remember any" (Terry). Once we make such an admission, we find that students accept the idea that social, political, economic, gender, race and cultural inequalities could be reduced to a great degree. They further agree that they should be reduced. If students are willing to adopt humanistic and liberal attitudes toward social, racial, economic, and gender equalities they need not be threatened by the more radical set of attitudes toward these concerns. It is simply another moment in quiet transformation. We take the thinking and commitment of our students seriously and build on their strengths. We organize our classroom teaching to reinforce their ideas that inequalities could be reduced to a great degree and extended into society. At the same time, we attempt to integrate Giroux's writings on these subjects.

In our discussions about Giroux's work we have identified some steps that Giroux takes in order to organize his material. For example, he (1) takes up a current issue, (2) describes it briefly, (3) describes how the right and the left create opposite practices, (4) tells us what is at stake (e.g., a historical truth and public memory), (5) explains the functions of the concepts that are at stake, (6) discusses how the "negative" side attacks the "positive" side in order to create a particular type of memory and truth, (7) provides details of the functions of what he considers are the "good" institutions in society from his own critical, moral and ethical perspective, (8) shows how other perspectives tend to undermine his visions, (9) justifies his vision of schools by justifying the kind of society he thinks we should create, (10) criticizes other visions of society, (11) talks about pedagogy, (12) talks about problems and conditions which hinder such a political project, and (13) tells us what needs to be done, where, and by whom to achieve such political goals. Since our aim is to integrate Giroux's writings into our course material as well as into our pedagogical practices, it makes sense to indicate the steps taken by Giroux to organize his material. This seems to make it easier for students to engage his writings. Another thing we have done to achieve integration is to select a specific set of Giroux's writings. We have selected a set of writings in which Giroux summarizes his arguments, critiques, analysis and pedagogical practices. Students find his summaries very helpful, and they have also proven to be convenient for us to use those point form summaries in our university classes.

Now we wish to describe how we organize our classroom teaching in order to use Giroux's work. Needless to say, over the years we have tried different ways of doing this. Here, we have chosen to describe the classroom organization that we have been practicing recently. We find the various activities that students undertake in our classes illustrates to them the significance of Giroux's critical pedagogy for their personal growth towards becoming reflective and critical teachers, cultural workers, and public intellectuals. "Aren't the ideas we're discussing just constructs of this time? Will there be a post-post-structuralist movement in a few years time?" (Jo).

Following Giroux's insights, we organize our classes around the concepts of student voice, safe-space, teacher authority, cultural capital of students and teachers, dominant and marginal discourses, problematizing the dominant discourses, reflection, reflection-in-action, producing local theories, student and teacher empowerment, and the role of schools and education in building a democratic society. We believe that teachers need to be able to ponder such questions as What counts as knowledge? What is worth teaching? What is the purpose and nature of instruction? and What is the school's role in society? Students are not always interested in asking such questions. There is almost always the mindset that claims that we, especially university teachers, should already know the answers. But these are not questions for "someone else;" they are the intellectual concerns of all teachers. If teachers are not encouraged and helped to deal with such questions, then they can only expect to be educational technicians.

In our courses we ask students to read assigned material, make notes, and then to build on these notes to give an approximately ten-minute presentation to the class. The presentation is followed by a-question-and answer period. At the end of each class, we ask students to write a reflection on what has happened that day. We encourage students to reflect-in-action, that is, to jot down notes or some points as they are listening to others or while they are talking to others. "These presentations are very useful. I find that once I read the chapter I remembered what the presenter said. It is much better to have us practice in front of our peers than to be lectured to" (Clark). When students have made their written reflections we then collect them. We highlight those points made by students which we think will enable them to ask further questions. Sometimes students want us to expand on some issues on which the discussion took place in the previous class. If this is the case, we prepare a short talk. The "minilecture" gives us a space to infuse our voices into the developing dialogue. When we conduct the next class, we start it by relaying to students the points they have raised in their reflections. The purpose is to recognize student voices and give them the significance they deserve. Sometimes, we ask students to share their reflections with others. Before we do this, we collectively decide if doing so in this instance is a good idea. Sometimes students do not feel comfortable with this format of self-disclosure, especially in the beginning of the semester. As students get to know each other, however, they become more comfortable with it. In fact, they enjoy listening to their peers reflection and claim that it helps them in their learning. If necessary, we share our "minilectures" with students and engage them in discussion. The purpose is to create a dialogue between students and the teacher. In doing so, we want to maintain our authority as teachers, while at the same time, attempting to re-duce the distance between teachers' authority and students' experiences. Ulti-mately, we want to create safe spaces where students can empower themselves. Students do not like long didactic lectures; therefore, in each class period there are two to four presentations by students in the class. These presenta-tions are normally followed by discussions and minilectures. "It was nice to have a lecture for a change. I wouldn't want it everyday because I find group discussions very interesting as well. I do enjoy being focused, however, and the lecture does provide some structure" (Niki).

In addition to short presentations and reflections, there are four to six group discussions. Students are asked to form groups of three to four students and discuss the set of readings they have completed. If there are four sets of readings, there will be four group discussions, and so on. The purpose of group discussion is to encourage students to voice their understanding of the readings based upon their own experiences, to experience self-disclosure, to build trust and alliances among their peers, to problematize the readings and to develop local theories, e.g., personal interpretations. Sometimes, when time permits, students in each group are asked to share their thinking with the whole class. On other occasions, one person from the group shares his/her group's thinking to the whole class. Each student gets a turn to speak on be-half of the group as the course progresses. One of the other agendas for this type of work is to make students responsible for the production of their own knowledge. One of the central aspects of our teaching is in the form of an in-dividual student-pedagogical project. Students need to be helped to produce rather than simply accept knowledge. As we wrote in the *Reading Giroux* part of this book, it is not easy for students who have been conditioned by transmis-sion to go beyond that form of learning. However, we believe that once stu-dents make this leap, they are more confident in taking responsibility for other aspects of their learning and for cultural practices in their communities. Therefore, it is not enough for us to simply tell students how to think. We have to try and go beyond that. Of course this is not easy for us as educators. We have been trained to be the ones who know. Once again, we have learned that there are many steps to any pedagogy of affirmation.

As part of an evaluation process, there are portfolios, paper folios, reflec-tion journals, and pedagogical papers and projects. The examinations, papers, or project questions are given to students well in advance of the official ex-amination date set by the university. Sometimes we ask students to write their own questions based on the assigned readings and classroom discussions. Often students raise insightful questions during their reflections, and we take these insights into account. These evaluation questions are discussed in the class. We try to make all such formal evaluations part of the learning. We do not treat them as following on the learning. Students are encouraged to develop their own unique answers by integrating concepts from assigned readings, personal experiences, and professional knowledge produced by others. "This course really has had a profound effect on the way I see things. I know you have taken a lot of flak for the workload in this course, but I found it to be manageable and challenging" (Trent). We emphasize to students the importance of writing. Students can make outlines of their papers and share them with us. The purpose here is to create safe spaces where students could get constructive feedback from their peers and from us. The purpose is to encourage a sense of building safe relationships among students and teachers, and to improve one's writing through the process of refining one's thoughts and through writing the answer two or three times over. We have to note that students, who do well on the first writing, do not always appreciate the fact that others get to rewrite. Individual competition remains a very real fact of university life. We try to keep Giroux's point of view about testing in mind. "Testing has become the new ideological weapon in developing standardized curricula; a weapon that ignores how schools can serve populations of students that differ vastly with respect to cultural diversity, academic and economic resources" (1993a, p. 16). We fully realize that no formal evaluation space is completely safe. In the end, students' work must be evaluated and assigned a grade. This is an institutional constraint that cannot be ignored given the way universities are set up at this time in history. We believe that if we can lock evaluation processes to learning then there is some balance to it all. However, like Giroux, we have to be careful that we are not being theoretically accurate but pedagogically wrong.

Another integral part of our course organization is to extend an invitation to each student to come and see us, phone us, or contact us by e-mail. While this process can make serious demands on time, it can have its own rewards. However, the simple purpose is to create another site where students and teachers can interact with each other. "I like how you always encourage us to ask questions, you have always been very positive in your responses to the people who have presented. There is nothing more wonderful than positive reinforcement" (Mal). This site, outside the classroom, can be helpful for individualized instruction. "I find the content is very difficult. I am a math major and critical thinking is not a big part of math. Problem solving is a big part" (Ted). Many students require mentoring. Mentoring is an art form involving communication. If students opt for this invitation, we try to ask them empowering questions that hopefully affirm their work and identity.

Graduate Research

We believe that one of the most significant sites that we work at is in the area of graduate research. Like other university professors we do this work in teaching courses on educational research and in supervising masters and doctoral students. This work is often taxing but very rewarding. We realize that often we are helping graduate students begin their own important research. We see the fruits of this work in solid papers, thesis and dissertations. We approach each course or supervision with a certain gentle apprehension. For we know that there is little doubt that there is increased diversity in how social research is approached and conducted. This diversity has lead to vastly expanded options for framing and carrying out educational research. A quick glance at the titles for papers presented at research conferences gives some indication of the array of approaches to educational research. This diversity is borne out by the range of thesis topics being encouraged and carried out at our particular university. We have to be prepared for such work. We also have to be prepared to help graduate students appreciate the significance and complexity of what they do. This often means trying to set a context for the ever-changing site of educational research.

There is also little doubt that the methodological and theoretical debate in education parallels a similar reassessment of dominant research approaches and methodologies underway in other academic areas. In many ways education is leading the way in this regard. Behind all of this development is the understanding that different modes of educational research involve different ways of examining the links between educational theory, practice, and change. No longer is research in education seen as a simple process of finding a solid method and applying it to everything that is studied. Education is much too complex for that. Discussions about research are very important in education, because of the struggles about what knowledge is important and who is to be authorized to speak about educational visions. Representation is always a hot topic in our discussions with graduate students. We try and instill the need to do respectful research.

In our discussions with graduate students we probe the relationship between educational research and educational practice as well as examine the different kinds of knowledge that we have access to. We investigate the place of theory and practice in education and emphasize that educational problems need to be researched in the social, cultural and historical context in which they emerge. We also stress that educational research should concern itself with values, judgments, and the interests of people. We recommend doing research with people and not on them. We always stress the claim that critical educational research is human, social, and political. We encourage discussions that interrogate prevailing educational structures and the political nature of schools and educational institutions. This often means a sharing of the contexts in which graduate students work and teach.

> My action research question focused on a new student who had enrolled in my class. His arrival seemed to change the dynamic of the teaching and learning occurring within my classroom context. When I began journal writing, his name appeared daily; whether he was in school or whether he was absent, his actions or his inactivity dominated my writing. Most journal entries seemed to underline my classroom management concerns as well as a developing frustration that focused on my seemingly unsuccessful attempts to reach and teach him. Instructional and classroom management strategies that I had deployed successfully in the past did not seem practical or effective with this particular student. I felt it necessary to analyze and evaluate my whole instructional approach to seek answers to my dilemma. (Katherine)

We want our students to know that critical educational research has the aim of transforming education and therefore is directed at educational change. Here is where we have our students use research questions based directly on their work situation or experience. In this way the information about educational research is not separate from their lives. This direct linking with students' real life situations has proved to be most effective in helping them understand the complexities of educational and social research. Often we ask our students who are enrolled in educational research courses to complete a major paper for the Critical Educational Research component of this graduate course. We always stress that students are free to choose any topic that might be of interest to them. They do make diverse and interesting choices: The makeup of School Councils; The focus on Achievement to Standards; The locus of Educational Achievement; The place of Parents in School Achievement; The rationale for the Extra High School Year; The future of Senior High School Special Education Students; The placement of Health in Core Areas; The relationship of Affective Outcomes to Academic Achievement; The significance of Specialized Schools; The relationship between Specific Core Subjects and Student Tolerance; The core placement of a Second Language; The place of Mindset in an Extended School Year; The focus of Essential Intellectual Skills and Capabilities; The factors that influence the Timing of Curricular Change; The significance of Difference in Classrooms; or The social and cultural aspects of Schoolyard Bullying.

We encourage graduate students to bring a critical lens to their topics by asking the questions like the following. In connection with your chosen research topic what relations among knowledge, power, and forms of domination would you need to critically examine? In relation to your research topic what social, cultural, political, economic, and historical sites and institutions would you need to probe? What ideological questions would you need to ask? How are the particulars of your research question linked to the larger factors of social, cultural, and economic realities? What educational values and beliefs stand behind any critical examination of your chosen topic? How do we get beneath the surface of institutional practices and structures that would have an impact on critically researching your topic? What elements of critical research would you use to guide your methodology in dealing with your chosen topic? What empirical work do we need to do to get at your research questions? In addition to the above topics and critical questions we examine key texts, issues, and methodologies within qualitative and critical educational research. These texts, issues, and methodologies are normally drawn from cultural studies, action research, critical ethnography, narrative inquiry, critical pedagogy, and feminist research. We do not believe that such reflection is automatic or easy. Our graduate students agree. "Journal writing, writing autobiographies, peer mentoring, discussion/study groups, collaborative problem solving, case study analysis, online discussion forums, and action research are but a few of the strategies that can enable teachers to purposefully reflect on their practice" (Kobie).

There was a time when many researchers would have denied that research is political. Today, the situation is different. There are, no doubt, still some who reject the idea that their work is political, but it is much more common to find declarations, or at least admissions, that it is. At the same time, claims that research is or should be objective, value neutral and nonpartisan are under attack. In the past, the denial that research is political was part of the assertion by social researchers of the scientific nature of their work, of its distinctiveness and authority, of its superiority to commonsense and practical experience. To a large extent claims to scientific rigour, objectivity and political neutrality were part of the process by which social science disciplines established themselves in institutional terms. In our discussions with graduate students we indicate that there is now greater emphasis on the fact that social and educational research cannot but be political. Until the middle of this century the positivist philosophy of science was most influential on social research. Giroux believes that separating knowledge and research from value claims often hides more than it uncovers. Giroux views the claims for objectivity are based on the use of normative criteria established by communities of scholars and intellectual workers in a given field. He further believes that it is impossible to achieve intellectual inquiry and research, which are free from values and norms. Giroux believes that it is pointless to separate values from facts or social inquiry from ethical considerations. We agree.

As we noted in the *Reading Giroux* part of this text, Giroux is very interested in the question about "the ways of producing knowledge and, more broadly, the validity of the distinction between legitimate intellectual knowledge and other kinds of knowledge" (Giroux & Aronowitz, 1991, p. 17). He points to the sacred place that quantitative methods of research have created for itself. He questions this place. We wrote earlier in this volume that the culture of positivism has traditionally set the parameters and values of educational research. Scholars working under the umbrella of positivism have limited what is accepted as worthwhile knowledge while marginalizing the valuable work of others. We, in this particular institution, have not been immune to positivism. We know, however, that if we do not protect our research, then our teaching will be of little value. We try to temper the forces of positivism by placing the possibilities of critical educational research before our students and colleagues.

We remind students that the early 1970s witnessed a gradual shift towards a more critical approach in educational research. Then the importance of social structural arrangements, power, ideology and social conflict, especially class conflict began to emerge in a powerful way. This research had concerns with everyday social interactions. Adequate attention was not being paid to differential power relations in such interactions. Traditionally researchers did not give proper consideration to the origins of power relations in structural divisions and conflicts. However, as a whole, the critical paradigm has offered alternative concepts for inclusion on the research agenda. These concepts include social structure, social conflict, regulation of social order, ideology, power and control along with class and gender. The methodologies of the emerging critical research tend to be qualitative, naturalistic and nonpositivist and include life history and other informal interviews, observational methods especially participant observation case studies and social history research. The central concepts and emphases of the critical paradigm raise key questions that can be examined by many forms including document and text analysis. These concepts include but are not limited to a concern with analysis at a societal and social structural level; an emphasis upon conflict between social groupings and on the dynamics of struggles between them; an emphasis on power and control in the relation between social groupings; an interest in ideology as a means by which existing structures and social arrangements are legitimated and maintained; a commitment to not taking for granted what-is-said; and a commitment to changing the existing state of things. We have found that when graduate students understand the evolution of educational research they are in a better position to have a context for their own work.

The comments in these pages are reflective of a critical-dialectical approach to social and educational research. The ideological and philosophical underpinnings of this approach are not taken for granted. We have spent considerable time, over the last number of years, trying to come to grips with our own little paradigm wars and our own philosophical security in such a discourse. While we believe we need to have general discussion on the nature, scope and delivery of graduate programs, we are also anxious that we make best use of the literature on the evolution of social and educational research. In many institutions, and ours is no exception, there is a continual, if polite, warfare about values and methodologies of social educational research. We find that this struggle never ends. We are also acutely aware that we are, to a large extent, talking about a struggle for academic agendas and ideologies. Part of what we want to do is improve the rigor and relevance of research in education by encouraging tolerance, reflection, and the utility of multiple approaches in knowledge production. We stress that it is reasonable for different persons to accept different interpretations and unreasonable to hope that one type of research can or should resolve all conflicts. In our interest with educational research we are informed by Henry Giroux's work in *Impure Acts, Beyond the Corporate University*, and *Take Back Higher Education*. McLaren and Giarelli write, "Giroux makes the production, texts, and practice of critical educational research themselves subjects of critical theory and educational research" (1995, p. 17).

When we stop to think about it, we can readily see that so much academic capital is at stake. We also find that there seems to be a correspondence with other battles in these halls. The resurgence of what we are calling neo-positivism is the catalyst for some of these paradigm wars. We have found it necessary to keep a critical perspective to the research supervision we do with graduate students. Once again, Giroux has been most helpful in this endeavour. Not so much for the particular methodological advice he offers but for the research questions he proposes. So much of the conceptual ground that Giroux covers is great material for social and educational research.

> By politicizing the notion of schooling, it becomes possible to illuminate the role that educators and educational researchers play as intellectuals who operate under specific conditions of work and who perform a particular social and political function. The material conditions under which teachers work constitute the basis for either delimiting or empowering their practices as intellectuals. (1988a, p. xxxii)

We believe that no one research paradigm is the best for all occasions. We need to realize that scientific, ethnographic, and critical modes of investigation each offer a worthwhile type of understanding. In our discussions we stress that what we are doing is not so much research methods as procedures that are given differential meanings within intellectual traditions or paradigms (McLaren and Giarelli, 1995). We readily admit that many of the differences in educational research are based on conflicting political and philosophical ideologies. However, there is a growing realization that the attempt to dispense with values, historical circumstances, and political considerations in educational research is misguided. Giroux claims, "Reducing theory to issues of verification and empiricism does not do justice to the issue of the historical connectedness between the language of theory and how it frames its objects" (McLaren and Giarelli, 1995, p. 28).

Our discussions with graduate students often center on such topics as positivism and antipositivism, the relationship between qualitative and quantitative research, the distinction between factual and value issues, as well as critical research. We indicate to students that part of the agenda of critical educational research is to explore the relations among knowledge, power, and domination and realize that schools, for example, are cultural and historical sites. It is not easy to decide what methods should be used to critique such complex relationships in educational research. For example, if we wished to examine the many facets of the "restructuring" and "reform" activities that are rampant at local levels in education, where would we start and what research means would we use? Would we be content to research discrete problems about the education system as if such problems were not somehow linked to the bigger factors of social, political, cultural, and economic realities? However, when we deal with such discrete problems we find that students can more readily see the links between the macro-and micro-issues. We also emphasize with graduate students that they have a responsibility to acknowledge that their research is not neutral. Reflexivity as it applies to critical research implies that the orientations of researchers will be shaped by their socio-historical locations, including the values and interests that these locations confer upon them. What this represents is a rejection of the idea that social research is, or can be, carried out in some autonomous realm that is insulated from the wider society and from the particular biography of the researcher, in such a way that its findings can be unaffected by social processes and personal characteristics. Also, we emphasize that the production of knowledge by researchers has consequences. Very often our graduate students do their research with students or teachers, and they can readily see what we are talking about. "Educators do not have a cookbook of proven recipes that work in every teaching and learning situation. The same could be suggested with regard to the most effective strategies that practitioners can apply to active reflection of their practice" (Kendra).

Critical educational research should always begin with the notion that existing social relations structure knowledge. Educational research should never be done in a vacuum. From a critical approach this simply does not make sense. Solutions to problems do not occur in a vacuum. We also stress that educational instances cannot be observed without reference to the shared educational values and beliefs of those involved with the critical research. We can only make sense of our research findings if they are placed against the background of a shared educational framework of thought. This is one of the reasons that solutions to educational problems must be produced and presented in their social, cultural, historical, economic, and political context. In addition to this, critical educational research should concern itself with the values, beliefs, judgments, and interests of the people involved with the particular research project. We have to remind ourselves that knowledge is never the product of a mind that is detached from the realities of daily concerns. Knowledge is produced out of human activity that is motivated by natural needs and interests.

We believe that it is part of our mandate in a progressive institution to allow and affirm the research directions of the critical, poststructural and postmodern. We, following on our own ideological foundations, try to indicate to graduate students the value of doing critical research. We remind graduate students that there are many ways of doing educational research. For example we talk about feminism as a critical approach to research; the political character of methods used; the political significance of a particular type of data; and ethical issues involved with certain kinds of research. This list of topics covers a wide variety of methodological issues. We need to ask ourselves: Can we produce accounts that correspond to the nature of social and educational reality? In many cases when we work with graduate students who are interested in critical questions, we begin with local educational issues that necessitate researching the political, cultural, social and economic contexts. One of our key agendas is to help students realize the vital connection between micro-and macro-issues. We also remind our graduate students that the theoretical and ideological frames that they bring to the inquiry are crucial. These theoretical and ideological frames cannot be dispensed with for they are the glasses through which we see the world.

One of the openings we look for in our work with students is to affirm teachers' voices through the use of narrative research. We stress that the nature of teachers' knowledge is often linked to teachers' narratives. This sometimes surprises graduate students. Explorations of what teachers know, how they think and learn professionally or how they make decisions in the classroom is a developing strand of research about teaching. Teachers' classroom knowledge can be thought of as high-context knowledge in the sense that most of the relevant information necessary to interpret what teachers say is either in the physical context or internalized in the person. When graduate students realize this they are helped to appreciate their own experience and their own voices. They learn to share and value their own personal practical knowledge. "Reflecting back on my years of teaching, I know that I have been successful in teaching my students some very valuable life lessons. Yet, at the same time, I realize there are many innovative approaches I could put into practice" (Vidi). Graduate students also learn the virtue of solving problems in specific situations and their descriptions of teaching, classroom management, and evaluation sound more like stories than theories. We also should note that the notion of teacher voice is very much linked with narrative research. The narrative account must therefore carry the teacher's voice if researchers and other observers are to know what a teacher knows or feels. This emphasis on voice and narrative also concurs with our agenda to encourage teachers to see themselves as researchers. That is why we put so much emphasis on action research.

In education, action research lies in the will to improve the quality of teaching and learning as well as the conditions under which teachers and students work in schools. Action research is intended to support teachers, and groups of teachers, in coping with the challenges and problems of practice and carrying through innovations in a reflective way. Many of the graduate students we work with are practicing teachers and invariably they are interested in transforming their own work sites. Action research is research by practitioners to solve their own problems and improve their professional practice. Educators from wide-ranging positions need to become researchers and self-reflective practitioners. We feel the need to share these ways of researching with our students. There is a need to stress the importance of understanding society from within, of interpreting social conduct in terms of cultural roles and norms and through the intentions, motives, emotions, and feelings of individuals. There is a need to present to our graduate students not only research that probes the effects of causal mechanisms but also the effects of negotiated rules and norms. We need to examine the social structures and agency. As Kincheloe states, "critical research is always conceived in relation to practice—it exists to improve practice" (McLaren and Giarelli, 1995, p. 74). This idea has great appeal for the graduate students we work with.

> Teachers are essential to the development of teaching and learning, however many feel that their input is often ignored or they lose interest because the "wheels of bureaucracy" turn so slowly. Teachers must know their learner or make a conscious effort to be informed as much as possible concerning their students. In doing so, they are the best to plan, teach, assess, and reflect on the assessment to help their students have meaningful learning experiences. The groups, outside of the classroom itself, who wield control and influence must learn to appreciate the role of the teacher in the learning process and appreciate their input. (Jennifer)

As we have noted many times in this project, Giroux sees great value in a closer working arrangement between education and cultural studies. When it comes to doing research, he is no less emphatic. He believes that a program that would utilize faculty from the different departments to teach interdisciplinary courses and to engage in collaborative research would be of great benefit. For example, he believes that "courses offered could be developed around themes like language and power in educational administration, reading educational psychology as historical texts, analyzing diverse curricula languages as a form of cultural production, analyzing pedagogy as an ethical discourse, and so on" (2005b, p. 195). It is very easy to see the significance this would have on research.

It is stating the obvious to claim that education itself is very complex. How could we expect less complexity from educational research? We have to realize that the challenge of critical analysis is extremely valuable to practicing educational researchers. Critical research dares us to look beyond common sense, to challenge accepted definitions, to uncover manifestations of hidden power, and to search for new and more appropriate methods of knowing more about education. In particular, graduate students as teacher researchers can seek a system of meaning that grants a new insight into the social consequences of different ways of knowing, different forms of knowledge, and different approaches to research. We have to realize that educational inquiry and the knowledge it produces is never neutral. This knowledge is often constructed in specific ways that privilege particular ways of thinking and certain people while it can often silence others. As we have indicated above, it is necessary to place many of these questions and problems in the larger systems of society, culture, politics, and economy. It is also obvious to see that claiming any one research approach can fully investigate all of these questions is to invite the wrath of Kuhn.

Cultural Production

In this section we move beyond the traditional borders of pedagogy to public pedagogy. We wish to share our attempt to integrate Giroux's work in our practice at the level of cultural production through drama. It is interesting for us to realize how easy it is to move from traditional pedagogical sites that are so familiar to the places of cultural production. It is also of interest to see how very portable the salient concepts of pedagogy transfer to cultural production. However, when we accept that the concepts of representation, power, ideology, and the like are so closely linked with both pedagogy and cultural production it is not hard to see why these borders are so readily crossed. Once again, the work of Henry Giroux has proven to be so very helpful.

For our purposes, in this articulation of Giroux's contribution to our work, we are limiting our use of cultural production to drama tand theatre. In contextualizing and describing this site, we are following Giroux's view of drama "as a pedagogical practice that links theory and practice, on
the one hand, and the politics of representation and the body on the other" (Doyle, 1993, p. ix). For purposes of simplicity, we are using the term theatre

to mean that drama which is put on stage. In this section of *Teaching Giroux* we will rely heavily on the concepts drawn from Giroux's work that deal with culture, society, representation, critical engagement, history, identity, power, ethical discourse, cultural politics, and cultural production. Once again, we only skim the surface of his multifaceted writings. We have come to realize, especially in recent years, just how much Giroux influences this type of cultural work.

Part of our agenda, influenced by Giroux, has been to link language, experience, affirmation, knowledge, and social responsibility. In other words, we have always seen the drama work we do as a process of critical engagement. Doing drama was always seen as political. The very nature of doing this type of cultural production cannot but be political. The personal interchanges and the varied roles played and played out in drama dictate that the process be political. The elements of power, knowledge, and the struggle for interpretation, constitute the political. As Giroux claims, we engage in plays as part of a broader attempt to understand ourselves, as well as our relationships with others. With drama we can also see how the dynamics of power operate in the intersection of life and fiction. Doing theatre, developing drama, and producing culture is an act of agency. One of the fascinations with doing such work is that it is done new each time. In fact, one of the conventions of theatre is that we give "the illusion of the first time" no matter how often the part has been played. This is one aspect of what Giroux calls the politics of representation. He claims that we need to engage each other in critical acts of cultural production. To do this we need to examine what interests stand behind the choice of play, the casting of roles, as well as the interpretation by the director. We need to "problemize the relationship between history, identity, and power [and deepen] the possibilities of an aesthetic that is at once critical, political, and emancipatory" (1993, p. x). Giroux believes that this form of cultural production can employ the critical categories of voice and difference in a way that links the private and the public, and that mark out our sense of place, culture, and community. We believe that this happens even if we do not plan it or are aware of it. In this way drama has the power to transform. Drama almost always speaks to us, about us, for us, or against us. Try as we will it is extremely difficult for us, in this process of cultural production, to separate the drama from configurations of ideology and power. No matter how much we choose to ignore the politics of theatre we are confronted by various representations

of identity construction, ethical considerations, and the interplay of domination, power, and agency.

> The play we did told a story that simply recognized our place on the planet and how
> that planet must be protected from our weakness, a counterpoint to our strength of
> theatre. Theatre makes us strong, individually and in groups. Not a politic many we
> know and work with can live with. It is dangerous because it challenges us all to find
> our humanness (Fred).

Following on Giroux, we believe that a cultural politics necessitates that a
discourse be developed that is attentive to the histories, dreams, and experiences of those presenting plays as well as those that absorb plays (1988a). By
valuing drama in this way, we have found that it is possible to produce meanings that engage, what Giroux calls, the contradictory forms of cultural capital.
Out of this engagement we can produce some form of meaning that speaks to,
and affirms, particular life experiences. We can use the process and the product of our cultural work, to fashion a new language where we can examine how
the power at work in plays is also at work in our lives. This then, can be part of
the vexing mix of resistance and hope.

We all operate with certain languages, ideologies, social processes, and
myths that, as Giroux claims, position us within existing relations of power
and dependency. Power is an active process within our lived relationships and
conditions. There is no better way, we believe, to probe that power, than
through the medium of drama. Giroux claims that power can be best understood through the experiences that we share in specific contexts and settings.
That is what drama does best. Giroux is also aware that "the symbolic presentations which take place in various spheres of cultural production in society
manifest contested and unequal power relations rooted in discursive and nondiscursive social forms" (1993a, p. 80).

We know that the complexity of our lives and the spaces we live in cannot
be fully represented by any play. Yet we do believe that we can get and give
glimpses of that reality. We know that we can point, and question, and sometimes even tell something about such lives and places. With drama, with its
many texts and representations, we can allow words and images speak about us
and to us. One of the plays that we have produced recently speaks to about the
demise of a single-industry factory town. This drama deals with one person's
struggle to maintain his dignity as he copes with the loss of his job, his family,
and ultimately, his freedom. The title for the play was taken from the lyrics of
a song: "Though we gave them our best years, now they've paid us back by

making us yesterday's men [sic]." These lines succinctly capture the essence of *Yesterday's Men*, which was meant to be a reflection of today's economic reality for many people. The play tells the universal story of the day-to-day struggle of shutdowns, moratoriums, loss of heritage, and the resulting human tragedy, as more and more of our people are consigned to the social scrap heap. Sadly enough it is indeed a story for our times; CNN attests to this claim. That play was conceived, written, and presented with the help of people who were living models for the characters in the play. It was their story. This was their cultural production. Many of the elements we have mentioned above, were systematically used as a conceptual foundation for this play. One of the most startling comments for us came from a community member who claimed "Nobody ever writes plays about us" (Gerry).

One of the things that we have come to do, on a regular basis, is to examine how people create stories, memories, and narratives. We have found ways to probe "the conscious and unconscious material through which members of dominant and subordinate groups offer accounts of who they are and present different readings of the world" (Giroux, 1988a, p. 106). In a very real sense, drama, in its many forms, is a wonderful medium for manipulating presented reality. Unlike film or visual art, a play is not fixed. It is fluid. It is open to incision, insertion, and inquisition. Giroux would say that it is one of those "ideologies and practices that allow us to understand the particular social locations, histories, subjective interests, and private worlds that come into play in any culture" (p. 106). In our cultural work, through drama, we are never content with simply presenting. We are never content with accepting the play at face value. We always ask: "What can we do with this play?" We are not willing to simply reproduce a play. We want to ask the cultural, social, historical, and political questions. These productions become, in a way, lived cultures. The process of researching, writing, and producing a play can easily take two years, and therefore does take on a life of its own. We are quick to add that we can afford this luxury, because we earn our livings in safer places. This form of cultural production can engage a particular personal or social circumstance through a process of confirmation and interrogation. Giroux is certainly right, when he says that the cultural work we select and produce must be interrogated critically in relation to expressed ideologies, personal representations, and social life. We have found that in order to do this we need to systematically, as part of the rehearsal time, to discuss, not only what is happening in the play, but also what is happening to us as we prepare it. We have become acutely aware that as in traditional pedagogical projects different people have different agendas. We have to work at respecting that intellectual and social reality. If plays are open to interpretation, it follows that they are open to different interpretations. Therefore, if a play is prepared and presented on a collegial basis, then the politics of the process comes to the front very quickly. We have to learn to work together in a fashion that not only probes but also transforms. It often becomes apparent that "the pedagogical dimension of cultural work reveals that the symbolic presentations which take place in various spheres of cultural production in society manifest contested and unequal power relations rooted in discursive and nondiscursive social forms" (Giroux, 1994, p. 64).

With our work there is a concern with the "analyses of the production and representation of meaning and how these practices and their effects are implicated in the dynamics of social power" (Giroux, 1993, p. 2). If we do not take this approach, then we will simply perform empty theatre. We believe that we have to be able to connect our own experiences to drama and capitalize on our own culture. This would seem to be a crucial link for the type of cultural production we are writing about here. We find that those who bring their own culture to drama can share that culture through drama. As indicated above, we try to leave room for this sharing in the process of discussion and rehearsal. Drama and culture are interdependent. The culture feeds the drama and the drama helps the culture. In rehearsals and in interpretation sessions, people can hold out their own histories and experiences for the group to see. Then they can be more confident to go back to their stories and use them to produce drama, their own drama. The personal as well as the cultural informs the drama processes, and invariably both show up in the production.

It is obvious that drama is a social force, and we need to use it as such. Most plays were not written on contract but were produced in a given culture to express some aspect of that culture. One such play that we researched, wrote, and produced recently was called *Out From Here*. This play was intended to show the unique cultural and historical bonds that exist between Ireland and Newfoundland. The play, while set in Newfoundland, is inextricably bound with the history and culture of Ireland. The story of "out-migration" as it happens in Newfoundland is linked with the "diaspora" that has been part of the Irish story. The story line begins with a farewell party for a Newfoundlander who is being forced to leave her once profitable business and community. The farewell party sets a story in motion that traces the migration of this individual's ancestors from Ireland to Newfoundland. While preparing to leave, Kathleen Kavanagh is given a mysterious painting. The painting depicts an Irish noblewoman and is marked 1750. This painting gives a theatrical convention that allows the story to move back and forth from Newfoundland to Ireland. This story crosses cultures, places, and times.

This play allows the audience to unravel the story of generations of one family that went from owning vast estates, to traveling the roads of Ireland, to emigrating to Newfoundland, to working for starvation wages, to owning a small business, to being quite prosperous, and now to outward migration brought on by the local economy. This story, like so many others about the people who came to North America, deals with a cross section of the Irish people that have come to Newfoundland over the decades and centuries, and who still go out from here. A play like this, gives tremendous opportunity to examine many of the concepts involved with a critical theatre. Many of these concepts were self-consciously borrowed from Giroux's work. In this particular instance, the cultural project closely matched the conceptual agendas we have in many traditional pedagogical projects. As Giroux and Aronowitz would claim, it is necessary for us to look for glimpses of emancipation. Seeing emancipatory possibilities even in fiction can be a source of encouragement and affirmation.

Another aspect of our Giroux-inspired work is done with schools and community drama groups. We have noticed that a large number of high-school students and teachers are writing and presenting their own plays. These plays usually grow out of the shared life of a community and are performed for the community and in this way become part of the produced culture of that community. This communal value alone speaks to the critical possibilities of drama because here we are not talking only about performance but about a process that is essential to cultural production. Drama in this instance is not simply a reflection of culture but a critical interaction with that culture and a production of culture.

A presented drama not only reflects the culture from which it grew but can help that culture change. Drama helps to produce or reproduce culture. We miss much of the potential for drama if we do not realize that it can play a part in reformulating culture just as it does in objectifying it. Drama is always produced and interpreted within given social conditions, yet it is not simply determined by such conditions. Drama, like other forms of art, must face up to the real world around it. There is interdependence between culture, economics, and drama. When we work with people on drama projects we try and look to the world of those involved in the cultural production and not limit themselves to plot, character, and form, which are important aspects of drama but are not necessarily transformative.

> A culture that does not see itself can not know itself. A culture that does not know itself can be lost without ever knowing it has been found. Theatre at its best is informative, engrossing light. It is the imaginative window through which we may view ourselves, and wonder at who we are, where we have been, what we can be. It is an opening, awaiting our entrance. (Michael)

Giroux remains a committed writer, prowling the frontiers of cultural and pedagogical theory. Behind much of his work must lay the belief that if we make it we can change it. For Giroux, the story is never over, the play is never finished, and the work is never done. One of the realities of doing intellectual and cultural work is that we never arrive. This can be daunting and frustrating. However, we have to remind ourselves that there are moments of empowerment and transformation; for ourselves and for our students. Giroux's sense of hope helps us toward those moments.

Giroux provides us with many insights about teaching, and we end this section with his thoughts.

> Teaching must be linked with empowerment and not merely with technical competence. Teaching is not about carrying out other people's ideas and rules without question. Teaching requires working within conditions in which power is linked to possibility, collective struggle to democratic reform, and knowledge to the vast terrain of cultural and social differences that map out the terrain of everyday life. (1993a, p. 26)

We have tried to take Henry Giroux's advice very carefully when he advocates the need to create the conditions and safe spaces that "offer teachers and students the opportunity to be border crossers as part of the effort to learn new languages, refiguring the boundaries of interdisciplinary discourse, and to consistently work to make the familiar strange and the given problematic" (1993b, p. 25). We appreciate this!

Reading Guide

Finally, another important part of course organization is the format we purposefully have used to select and group the writings of Giroux. We have put these selected writings into seven sets. The rationale for organizing the readings in this particular format is pedagogical. The special feature of this format is that each set contains the Giroux writings that match our particular teaching agenda. Our only claim here is that the writings chosen enable us to integrate Giroux's insights in our courses more strategically. We ask readers to note that under the title selected for a particular set, we identify various theories and concepts that Giroux uses to develop his narrative as he makes his arguments. The concepts we have identified under each article give a bird's eye view to what one would find in that article. In other words, the format serves as an overview to the complete article, and in this way it approximates a ready-made instructional outline. Another feature of the readings listed is that we have selected certain pages from Giroux's writings where he summarizes key ideas. In our informal observations in the classroom and during conversations with students we have noticed that students see those summaries as ready-made notes and find them useful to develop their own thoughts, term papers, and pedagogical projects. Also, when students and colleagues see material arranged in this format, they get focused on the subject matter covered by Giroux and others. This readily facilitates conversations among students and colleagues.

Set One

Autobiographical Sketches

1. Giroux in *Border Crossing*

    • Shift in Giroux's politics and his theoretical work • Teacher education and public schools still crucial sites for critical citizenship • Underestimation of both the structural and ideological constraints under which teachers labor • The ravages inflicted by federal and state policies on education during the Reagan/Bush Era • Factors reducing the influence that critical educators might play as public intellectuals • The shift away from pedagogy as dehistoricized, theoretical practice • Pedagogical practice as a form of cultural politics • The use of language • Teachers are not "too dumb" to read theoretical books • What pedagogy actually is and does • Demand of a rewriting of the meaning of pedagogy • Politics of erasure in the Bush Era • Rise of a new form of McCarthyism • The debilitating effects of Eurocentric perspectives on identity and difference • The concept of "cultural worker"

2. Giroux in *Between Borders*

•The field of cultural studies and critical pedagogy • Issues regarding representation and the discourse of difference, desire and the pedagogy of commodification, cultural memory and the politics and cultural work, democracy and the discourse of the border intellectual, and eros and the politics of reception

3. Giroux in *Disturbing Pleasures*
•Growing up in a working-class neighborhood in Providence, Rhode Island • Popular culture and schooling • My friends talked, danced, and lost ourselves in a street culture • The school and me • The culture of print • Disc, male prerogative and sport • The language • The working-class kids in my school • What happened to my friends • Escape into a middle-class world • Return to my own sense of home and identity • Pedagogy is not a discipline • Pedagogy is about the creation of a public sphere • Electronic media

4. Giroux in *Channel Surfing*
•The Reagan - Bush period beginning in the 1980s • A broader dialogue in understanding the current circumstances shaping the lives of young people • The category of youth • Youth as lived experience • The formative conditions of my own youth as it was lived in the late fifties and early sixties • Race and class division • A different set of circumstance for today's youth • The threat of dead-end jobs, unemployment, and diminished hopes confront today's youth • Hip-hop culture • What is meant to be a white male • Whiteness and maleness • My working-class neighborhood • Individual and collective identities • Interaction with "others" were violent • Segregation was the order of the day • Community was defined within racial and class differences • Solidarity was mostly based on the principle of exclusion • College students and us • Had no contact with middle-class and ruling-class kids until we went to high school • The working-class black and white kids and the rich white kids • Basketball in my life • Racial and class differences fueled by bigotry, intolerance, and systemic inequalities were the disruptive forces in my life • An attempt to engage in a form of memory-work • Education works best when those experiences that shape and penetrate one's

lived reality are jotted, unsettled, and made the object of critical analysis

Set Two

Biographical Sketches

5.   Paulo Freire's commentary on Giroux and his work
   • Giroux as a thinker and an excellent professor • Complex relationships among objects • History as a possibility • The unquestionable role of subjectivity in the process of knowing

6.   Stanley Aronowitz's commentary on Giroux and his work
   • The United States as the leading imperial power • Socialism • Education as the great democratic institution • Education for self-improvement • American capitalist democracy • American education as a route to social mobility • Failure of schools to obliterate class inequality • Schools linkage to the industrial order • Schools as more than ideological apparatus • Scientific management • The degradation of labor in the 20th century • Critical research on school in the United States • Giroux's work as critique of the functionalist assumptions of both liberal publicists and radical critics of American education • Giroux's major contribution to educational theory • Giroux performing the work of immanent critique • The principle of hope • The school is a terrain of contestation rather than an ideology machine • Giroux's contribution to the critical theory of education and social theory

7.   Peter McLaren - *Henry Giroux's Pedagogy of the Concrete*
   • Schooling and its Relationship to the Wider Society • The Generative Foundations for a Critical Social Theory of Schooling • New Advances in Social Theory and New Categories of Theoretical Inquiry • Schools Function as One of the Major Mechanisms for the Development of the Democratic and Egalitarian Social Order • The Analysis of the Neoconservative Resurgence in Education • The Logic of the Excellence Movement in Education • The Criticisms of Progressives in Education • Institutionalized Tracking and Structuring the Curriculum • Political and Pedagogical Accomplishment of Giroux • The Structured Inequality of Competing Self-Interests

Within a Social Order • The Fundamental Public Services Associated With Schooling in American Society • The Political Forms of Contemporary Schooling • The Limitations and Historical Contingency of Theory Itself • Giroux's Critical Thought as Part of an Ongoing Project of Pedagogical Struggle and Political Empowerment • Cultural Studies • The Imperative of Empowering Students • The Central Issue is the Development of a Language for Educators for Transforming the Larger Social Order • The Dominant School Culture • Hegemonic Practices That Often Silence Subordinate Groups • A Passion and Indignation in Giroux's Writings • A Militant Hope in Giroux's Writings • The Capacity of Human Agents to Remake the World • Teaching as a Form of Cultural Politics • Teaching as a Pedagogical Enterprise That Takes Seriously Relations of Race, Class, Gender, and Power in the Production and Legitimation of Meaning and Experience • A Series of Questions Which Have Guided Giroux's Work • Periods to Giroux's Work: First, (late 1970s) The Concept of Culture Had to be Politicized and Theories of Social and Cultural Reproduction had to be Challenged • Second, (early 1980s) The Issue of Agency and Student Resistance Needed to be Considered • Ideology • The Transformative Possibilities of Experience • Classroom Knowledge • Teacher Must Make Knowledge and Experience Emancipatory • Civic Courage • The Concept of Schools as Democratic Public Spheres • Democracy • The Issue of Language • The Concept of Power/Knowledge and Teachers as Intellectuals • Giroux's View on Scholarly Writing • Giroux's Notion of Schooling as a Form of Cultural Politics • Pedagogy • A Pedagogy of the Concrete • Instrumental Practice and Empowering Practice

8.   Joe L. Kincheloe, Peter McLaren and Shirley R. Steinberg's commentary on Giroux's work.

•Giroux as the most creative educational thinker • Giroux and the struggle for a radical democracy • Giroux's trademark language of critique and possibility • Giroux's analysis of Reaganism • Giroux's introduction of Frankfurt school critical theory into the discourse of educational scholarship • Giroux's ability to name ways in which power operated to undermine the dignity and mobility of marginalized students • Giroux ability to demonstrate power of social theory • Giroux's ability to unmark forms of domination • The relationship among power, ideology, and schooling • The culture of positivism • The distinction between the culture of positivism as ideological form and positivism as a specific philosophical movement • Schools a site of oppression • The self-determination (agency) and construction of student and teacher subjectivities • Giroux's appreciation of poststructuralist contribution to social theory • Giroux's insights concerning modes of reception and mediation • Giroux's fascination with British cultural studies • Giroux's conceptualization of power as a concrete set of practices • Giroux analysis of the critical postmodern feminist theory • Giroux's use of the post-colonial critiques of the Eurocentric position • Giroux's version of a critical postmodern and multicultural pedagogy • Giroux's critical pedagogy and issues of difference • Construction of race, class, and gender identities of students and teachers • Giroux's focus on the pedagogical terrain of power, knowledge production and transmission in relation to the referent of a radical democracy • Cultural studies and popular culture as legitimate areas of academic studies • Giroux's refocused concern with cultural studies and radical democracy • Giroux's 1990s understandings of the pedagogical process, new insight into pleasure, new maps of desire, and fresh interpretations of relationship among reason, emotion, and domination.

Set Three

Interviews

9.   David Trend - *Critical Pedagogy and Cultural Power: An Interview With Henry A. Giroux*

•The Language of Critical Pedagogy • The New Paradigms That Pedagogical Language Conveys • Marxism • The Reagan Administration • Allan Bloom, E.D. Hirsch Jr., Dian Ravitch, John Silber, Chester Finn Jr., and William Bennett • Trilateral Commission Study of 1965 • Turning Democracy on its Head • What "Taken Up" Means? • Struggle and Democracy • Theories of Schooling and Cultural Politics • The Right Left Cultural Workers • The Language of Teacher Education • The Ideology of Positivism • Authority and Agency • The Problem of Authority • The Power of the Public Intellectuals • Teachers and Communities • Cultural Workers • The Fight for Curricular Democracy • Schools as Political Sites • The Need to Broaden the Definition of Culture and Political Struggle • Discursive Spaces • Why Pedagogy is Both Exhilarating and Dangerous

10. *The Hope of Radical Education: A Conversation With Henry Giroux*
• Radical Education • Radical and Critical • Empowerment • Democracy • The Dominant Language of Education • Critical Democracy • Pedagogy and Power • Marxism and Radical Education • Marxist Discourse • Ideology and Language • Transformative Intellectuals • Schools of Education • Student Voice • Giroux's Teaching Style • Giroux's Educational Philosophy

11. Lech Witkowski - *Traveling Pedagogies*
• Collaborative Work • The Basic Definition (Giroux's) Idea of Pedagogy • People's Reaction Toward the Notions of Radicalism or Criticism • How to Avoid Accusations of Being an Extremist • Struggle • Authoritarian Knowledge • Pedagogy Without Any Self-Criticism • Traditional Pedagogical Concerns • Issues of Objectivity, Autonomy, and Consensus • Intellectual Work • What It Does • Science and Objectivity • The Ability to Imagine the "Not-Yet" • Individual Consciousness, Action and Promise of Solidarity in Struggle • Hard and Soft Notion of Oppression • Neoconservative and Neoliberal Streams of Pedagogy in America • Human Abilities • Culture • Curriculum • Canon • Popular Culture • Language • The Concept of "Emancipatory Authority" • "Civic Courage" • "Public Sphere" • Transformative Intellectual • How To Teach Teachers • The Term of "Border" • "Border Pedagogy" • The Idea of "Crossing Borders" • The Concept of Homelessness • Giroux's Teaching Style

Set Four

Giroux and Language

12. Henry A. Giroux - *Language, Power, and Clarity or "Does Plain Prose Cheat"*

•Social Criticism • Feminist Theory • Literary Studies • Art Criticism • Postcolonial Analysis • Afro-American Cultural Criticism • The Status Quo • Opaque Writing • Anti-Intellectualism in American Life • The Call for Clarity • The Politics of Clarity • "Utopian" Writing • The Attack on Language - Conservative, Liberal, Marxists • The Complicated Discourses • Vanguard Theories • Readability Theories • Curriculum Theorists and Attack on Critical Educators • Populist Elitism • The Issue of Language Around a Politics of Difference • The Relationship Between Theory and Practice • The Public Debate About Curriculum Issues • Universal Standard • Populist Prose • An Objectively Verifiable Reality • The Reproductive Model and the Reproduction Thesis of the Curriculum Theorist • Language and its Revealing or Demystifying Function • A Language of Negotiation and Translation • A Role of Theory Beyond the Task of Demystification • The Active Role of Language • Uses of Language to Generate New Theories and Point Alternative Territories of Investigation • Critical Public Cultures of Resistance and Political Practice • Questions of Validity, Verifiability, and Explanation • Language as Theoretical Discourse • An Emancipatory, Self-Reflective Notion of Theory as Resistance and Struggle • Theory Construction • Eurocentric Privileges • Language and Power • An Essentialist Notion of Clarity • Public Cultures of Resistance • A Universal Standard of Literacy • Questions of Context • Neocolonial Paranoia • Language as a Terrain of Contestation and Struggle • A Unified Single Standard of Writing and the Search for a Unified Identity, Politics, and Notion of Truth • Multiple Languages and Democratic Possibilities • Linguistic Diversity and Cultural Democracy • Oppositional Paradigms and New Languages • The Relationship Between Language and the Notion of Domination • The Homogenization and Standardization of Language in Mass Media, The School, and other Cultural Sites • An Audience and Audiences • One Public Sphere and a Number of Public Spheres • The Specificity of the Audience and Construction of a Language • An Effort to Redefine the Relationship Between Politics, Pedagogy, and Collective Struggle • Deepening and Extending Democracy and Social Justice in the Wider Society

Set Five

Critical Theory of Education

13. Barry Kanpol - *Critical Theory and Critical Pedagogy*
•Control • Critical Theory • Postmodernism • Democracy • Hegemony • Counter Hegemony • Authoritarianism • Deviance • Resistance • Deskilling • Authority • Reskilling • Multiculturalism • Traditional Empowerment • Critical Empowerment • Traditional Literacy • Critical Literacy • Individualism • Individuality • Negative Competition • Positive Competition

14. Henry A. Giroux - *Teacher Education as Cultural Politics*
•Power • Language • History • Culture • A Critical Pedagogy for the Classroom • The Primacy of Student Experience • Student Voice and the Public Sphere

Set Six

Giroux's Teaching Style

15. Giroux in *Disturbing Pleasure*
16. Giroux in *Border Crossing*
17. Giroux in *Pedagogy and the Politics of Hope*
•Symbolic violence • An apparent contradiction that lies at the heart of teaching • The contradiction between being theoretically or politically accurate and pedagogically wrong at the same time • Creating a safe space for students • Provide students with variety of texts • No endless lectures on the virtues of the working class • Concept of the political • How the operations of power and ideology work in schools • The relationship between class, race, sexism • Issues concerning the state, the politics of representation and hip political correctness • Engaging in writing, talking, and reading a variety of texts • Summary of three things Giroux does in his teaching • Student voices

Set Seven

Other Selected Writings Giroux

18. Henry A. Giroux - *Cultural Studies and Youth: The Pedagogical Issues*
   •A Postmodern Generation of Youth • Modernist Version of Representation of Schooling • An Emerging Postmodern Discourse • The Electronic Media • Culture and Power • Knowledge and Authority • Learning and Experience • The Role of Teacher as Public Intellectual • Critical Pedagogy • Cultural Studies • Cultural Work

19. Henry A. Giroux - *Critical Pedagogy and the Discourse of Cultural Politics (Teacher and Students as Transformative Intellectuals*
   •Cultural Politics • Transformative Intellectuals • Pedagogy of Cultural Practice

20. Henry A. Giroux - *Education and the Discourses of Production, Text Analysis, and Lived Cultures*
   •Objective Conditions Within Which Schools Function: The State • The Workplace • Foundations • Publishing Companies • Other Political Interests

21. Henry A. Giroux - *Liberal Discourse and Educational Practice*
   •Liberal Theory as the Ideology of Deprivation • Liberal Theory as the Pedagogy of Cordial Relations • Liberal Theory and the Pedagogy of Child Centeredness • Dominant Education Discourses

22. Henry A. Giroux - *Critical Pedagogy as a Form of Cultural Politics*
   •Critical Pedagogy and a Form of Cultural Politics (Paulo Freire and Mikhail Bakhtin) • A Pedagogy of Cultural Politics • Educational Practice and the Discourse of Production • Critical Pedagogy and the Discourse of Textual Analysis • Critical Pedagogy and the Discourse of Lived Cultures

23. Henry A. Giroux - *Beyond Textual Critique: Developing a Notion of Culture and Political Struggle Informed by a Particular Language*

• Cultural Democracy • Cultural Workers • Historical Memory • Representational Practices • Cultural Practice • Cultural Work • Prophetic Criticism • Language of Imagination

24. Henry A. Giroux - *A Liberatory Theory of Border Pedagogy*

• Difference • Voice • Politics • Democracy • Schools • Democratic Public Spheres • Critical Citizenship • The Struggle for Equality and Justice • Everyday Life • A Hierarchy of Struggles • A Politics of Solidarity • Political Community • Postmodern Citizenship • Cultural Remapping as a form of Resistance • Dominant Culture • Narratives, Languages, and Experiences for Boarder Crossing • Diverse Cultural Histories and Spaces • Identity • The Master Narrative • Borderlands • Sites • Critical Analysis, Experimentation, Creativity and Possibility • Dominated and Subordinated Subjects • Dominant, Historical, Ideological, and Institutional Mechanisms • The Pedagogical Borderlands • Dual Sense of Power • Power and Authority • Teacher Authority • A Pedagogy of Affirmation • Various Structures of Meaning and Practice • Establishing Conditions of Learning • Reading Texts Oppositionally • Writing One's Own Narratives • The Syntax of Learning and Behavior Outside of the Geography of Rationality and Reason • Making Ideological and Affective Investments in Narratives • Interaction of Meaning and Pleasure • Restructuring the Curriculum • The Discourses of Cultural Studies

25. Henry A. Giroux - *A Notion of Border Pedagogy and Basic Elements of Antiracist Pedagogy*

• The Conservative Notion of Democracy • The Logic of the Market • The Ideology of Cultural Uninformative • Radical Democracy • Rethinking the Relations Between the Centers and the Margins of Power • The Basic Elements of An Antiracist Pedagogy • A Border Pedagogy of Postmodern Resistance • A Border Pedagogy and the Perspective of the Subject Positions • Forms of Authority Rooted in Democratic Interests and Emancipatory Social Relations • The Everyday Experience of Marginality and Oppositional and Transformative Consciousness Empowerment • Initiation into the Culture of Power • The Authority of White Dominant Culture •

Egocentric Culture • A Postmodern Notion of Authority • The Circuits of Power and Various Sites of Cultural Production • Role of Teachers to Fight Racism

26. Henry A. Giroux - *A Critical Pedagogy*
•The Relationship Between the Pedagogical and the Political Social Movement • Emancipatory Struggles and Social Transformations • Some Basic Principles • Meaning of Education • Critical Democracy • Critical Citizenship • Critical Pedagogy • Ethics • Difference • Need for a Language that Allows for Competing Solidarities and Political Vocabularies • Needs to Create New Forms of Knowledge • Breaking Down of Disciplinary Boundaries • The Reformulation of the Enlightenment Notion of Reason • Need a Sense of Alternative • Need to Combine a Language of Critique and Possibility • Need to Develop a Theory of Educators and Cultural Workers as Transformative Intellectuals • Politics of Voice

27. Henry A. Giroux - *A Language of Critique and Possibility*
•A Language of Historical Perspective • The Language of Social Criticism • The Language of Remembrance • A Language of Critical Imagination

28. Henry A. Giroux - *Democracy*
•Democracy is a Terrain of Struggle • Democracy as a Practice is Noisy and Agnostic • There Exists More Than One Conception of Social Justice and the Public Good • Preconditions for Democracy • Citizenship as a Postmodern Concept

29. Henry A. Giroux - *Teachers as Cyborgs*
•Improving Teacher Education • Developing Closer Links Between Schools of Education Faculty and Teachers in the Public Schools • Teachers and the Dominant Pedagogical Models • The Current Reform Movement • America 2000

30. Henry A. Giroux - *Testing and the New Illiteracy*
•America 2000 • Standards and Tests • A National Curriculum • National Testing and a Standardized Curriculum • Measuring

Intelligence, Knowledge, and Skills • Tracking • The Discourse of Educational Change • Cultural Diversity • Disempowering and Deskilling Teachers • Accountability • Self-Identity, Culture, Power, and History • Cultural Democracy, Critical Citizenship, and Basic Human Rights • Training of Education Leaders in the Language of Management, Measurement, and Efficiency • Child Poverty, Unemployment, Illiteracy, Health Care, Sexism, and Racial Discrimination

31. Henry A. Giroux - *The Difficulty of Difference*
    •Identity Politics • An Undifferentiated, Whole, Stable, and Autonomous Self • The Old Left of Orthodox Marxism • The New Left • The Discourses of Authenticity, Experience, and the Personal • Political Moralism • The Politics of Personal Location • The Danger of Essentialism and Separatism • A Politics of Representation

32. Henry A. Giroux - *An Emancipatory Theory of Leadership*
    •The Task of Creating a Public Language • Administrators and Teachers in Schools of Education and Leadership • Educating for Democracy • Schools as Democratic Public Spheres • Need to Create the Conditions and Safe Spaces for Teachers and Students

33. Henry A. Giroux - *Pedagogical Authority and the Politics of the Popular*
    •Subject Positions of Students • A Dominant Eurocentric Assemblage of Liberal Humanism • The Film as a Mode of Writing and the Pedagogical Challenge

34. Henry A. Giroux - *Reclaiming the Popular*
    •The Popular • The Popular and Reaffirming the Textual Authority • Humanistic Discourses and the Popular • The Risk of Colonizing the Popular • Cultural Workers • The Role of Educators • Significance of Having a Political Project • A Political Project

35. Henry A. Giroux - *Toward a Pedagogy of Representation and Representational Pedagogy*

•Cultural Workers • The Politics of Representation • A Critical Pedagogy of Representation • A Critical Representational Pedagogy • Difference and Identity • Images, Sounds, and Texts • Photographic, Aural, and Televisual Culture • Questions of Subjectivity, Power, and Politics

36. Henry A. Giroux - *Modernism, Postmodernism, and Feminism*
•The Theoretical Status and Political Viability of Various Postmodern Discourses • Debate Among Diverse Feminist Groups • Feminist Discourses Influenced by Postmodernism • A Theory and Practice of Transformative Feminism • Democratic Struggles • The Primacy of Social Criticism • Rejecting the Postmodern Emphasis on Erasing Human Agency • Asserting the Importance of Difference • The Primacy of the Political • The Problematization of Gender Relations

37. Henry A. Giroux - *The Kids Aren't Alright: Youth, Pedagogy, and Cultural Studies*
•A Concept of Youth • Giroux's Own Journey Through an Adult World

38. Henry A. Giroux - *Ritualistic, Symbolic, and Hyper-Real Violence*
•The Representation of Violence in Media Culture •Educators and Representational Violence • Analyzing Visual Violence • The Pedagogical Consequences of Ritualistic Violence • Representations of Violence and Representations of Race

39. Henry A. Giroux - *Cultural Pedagogy and Children's Culture*
•Disney and Children's Culture • How Cultural Workers, Educators, and Parents Engage Disney's Influence of Children

40. Henry A. Giroux - *Higher Education as a Public Sphere*
•The Concept of the Public • Debates About Education • The University is a Major Public Sphere • The Role of the Progressive Cultural and Educational Workers • The Pedagogy of the Political Education • Meaning of a Political Education • A Politicizing Education • Public Intellectuals • Critical Educational Work • The De-

velopment of an Educational Policy • An Antiracist Struggle and the Relationship Between Schooling and National Identity • Educators and "Patriotic" Youth Culture • Educators and Media Culture • Cultural Studies and Public Life • Cultural Studies and the Education of Citizens

41. Henry A. Giroux - *Cultural Work and Radio Pedagogy*
    •Progressives and the Rise of Conservative Public Intellectuals • Public Intellectuals and Forms of Cultural Authority • Civic Life • Educational Workers, The Conservative Assault on Civic Culture and Resistance • Left Scholars as Public Intellectuals • The Concept of the Public Intellectuals in the United States • Black Intellectuals • A Model of the Populist Public Intellectual and the Right Wing • The Pedagogical Value of Talk Radio as a Medium and Issues of Race and Youth

42. Henry A. Giroux - *The Politics of Standards*
    •"Political Correctness Debate" • The Canon • The "Other" • An Insistence on "Excellence" • The Defining Principle of Traditional Pedagogical Practice • The Conservatives and the Content of Traditional Education

43. Henry A. Giroux - *Politics and Education*
    •The Relationship Between Authority and Teaching • What Counts as Legitimate Knowledge, Culture, History and Speech • The Conservative View of Knowledge • Politicized Teaching and Teaching Politics.

44. Henry A. Giroux - *Cultural Studies and Youth: The Pedagogical Issues*
    •The Emergence of a Postmodern Generation of Youth • Advertisers and Market Research Analysts and Youth • Educators and the Need to Make the Pedagogical More Political • Modernist Versions of Schooling • Popular Culture • The Emergence of the Electronic Media • The Effects of Emerging Postmodern Conditions on the Current Generation of Youth • The Field of Cultural Studies and Educators

45. Henry A. Giroux - *Intellectual Vocations and Public Celebrities*
•What it means for academics to have critical relationship to the public • The vocation of intellectual life • Inserting the category of the political back into the vocation of intellectual life • Task of academics is to weaken the boundaries between the disciplines and between the university and society • Interrogating how knowledge is produced, circulated, and applied • The test of social relevance • The public • The measure of the public intellectual • Defining public intellectual

References to Reading Guide

Set One
Autobiographical Sketches of Henry A. Giroux

1. Giroux, H. (1993). Introduction. In H. Giroux, *Border crossings: Cultural workers and the politics of education* (pp 1–5). New York: Routledge.

2. Giroux, H., and McLaren, P. (1994). Acknowledgments. In H. Giroux and P. McLaren (Eds.), *Between borders: Pedagogy and the politics of cultural studies*. New York: Routledge.

3. Giroux, H. (1994). Preface. In H. Giroux, *Disturbing pleasures: Learning popular culture* (pp. ix-xi). New York: Routledge.

4. Giroux, H. (1997). Race and the Truance of Youth. In Giroux, H. (1997). *Channel surfing: Race talk and the destruction of today's youth* (pp. 4–14). New York: St. Martin Press.

Set Two
Biographical Sketches of Henry A. Giroux

5. Freire, Paulo in Giroux, H. (1988). Teachers as intellectuals: Toward a critical pedagogy of learning (pp. xxvii–xxviii). New York: Bergin and Garvey.

6. Aronowitz, S. (1981). Preface. In H. Giroux, *Ideology, culture and the process of schooling* (pp. 1–4). Philadelphia: Temple University Press.

7. McLaren, P. (1988). Forward: Critical theory and the meaning of hope. In H. Giroux, *Teachers as intellectuals: Toward a critical pedagogy of learning* (pp. ix-xxi). Massachusetts: Bergin and Garrey Publishers, Inc.

8. Kincheloe, J., McLaren, P., and Steinberg, S. (1997). Series Editors' Foreward. In H. Giroux, *Pedagogy and the politics of hope: Theory, culture and schooling - A critical reader* (pp. ix-xiv). Colorado: Westview Press.

Set Three
Interviews with Henry A. Giroux

9. Trend, D. (1993). Critical pedagogy and cultural power: An interview with Henry A. Giroux. In H. Giroux, *Border crossings: Cultural workers and the politics of education* (pp. 149-160). New York: Routledge.

10. Giroux, H. (1993). The hope of radical education: A conversation with Henry Giroux. In H. Giroux, *Border crossings: Cultural workers and the politics of education* (pp. 9-18). New York: Routledge.

11. Giroux, H. (1994). Traveling pedagogies. In H. Giroux, *Disturbing pleasures: Learning popular culture* (pp. 153-171). New York: Routledge.

Set Four
Giroux and The Language Issues

12. Giroux, H. (1993). Language, power, and clarity or "does plain prose cheat?" In G. Giroux, *Living dangerously: Multiculturalism and the politics of difference* (pp. 155-171). New York: Peter Lang Publishing, Inc.

Set Five
Some Major Concepts In The Critical Theory of Education

13. Kanpol, B. (1994). Teachers' lives in a period of crisis: Tensions of meaning. In B. Kanpol, *Critical pedagogy: An introduction* (pp. 25-59). Connecticut: Bergin and Garvey.

14. Giroux, H. (1988). Teacher education as cultural politics. In H. Giroux, *Schooling and the struggle for public life* (pp. 188-202). Minneapolis: University of Minnesota Press.

Set Six
Henry A. Giroux's Teaching Style

15. Giroux, H. (1994). *Disturbing pleasure: Learning popular culture.* New York: Routledge (pp. 168-171).

16. Giroux, H. (1993). *Border crossing: Cultural workers and the politics of education.* New York: Routledge (pp. 16-17).

17. Giroux, H. (1997). *Pedagogy and the politics of hope:* Theory, culture, and schooling - A critical reader (p. 171). Colorado: Westview Press.

Set Seven
List of Other Selected Writings of Henry A. Giroux

18. Giroux, H. (1996). Cultural studies and youth: The pedagogical issue. In H. Giroux, *Fugitive cultures: Race, violence, and youth* (pp. 46-54). New York: Routledge.

19. Giroux, H. (1988). Critical pedagogy and the discourse of cultural politics. In H. Giroux, *Teachers as intellectuals: Toward a critical pedagogy of learning* (pp. 100-102). New York: Bergin and Garvey.

20. Giroux, H. (1988). Education and the discourses of production, text analysis, and lived cultures. In H. Giroux, *Teachers as intellectuals: Toward a critical pedagogy of learning* (pp. 102-107). New York: Bergin and Garvey.

21. Giroux, H. (1991). Liberal discourse and educational practice. In H. Giroux, *Schooling and the struggle for public life: Critical pedagogy in the modern age* (pp. 125-132). Minneapolis: University of Minnesota Press.

22. Giroux, H. (1991). Critical pedagogy as a form of cultural politics. In H. Giroux, *Schooling and the struggle for public life: Critical pedagogy in the modern age* (pp. 132-146). Minneapolis: University of Minnesota Press.

23. Giroux, H. (1993). Writing against the empire. In H. Giroux, *Border crossings: Cultural workers and the politics of education* (pp. 247-248). New York: Routledge, Chapman and Hall.

24. Giroux, H. (1993). Cultural studies and resisting difference. In H. Giroux, *Border crossings: Cultural workers and the politics of education* (pp. 174–176). New York: Routledge, Chapman and Hall, Inc.

25. Giroux, H. (1993). Beyond the politics of pluralism. In H. Giroux, *Border crossings: Cultural workers and the politics of education* (pp. 135–141). New York: Routledge, Chapman, and Hall, Inc.

26. Giroux, H. (1993). Modernism, postmodernism, and feminism. In H. Giroux, *Border crossings: Cultural workers and the politics of education* (pp. 73–80). New York: Routledge, Chapman and Hall, Inc.

27. Giroux, H. (1993). A language of critique and possibility. In H. Giroux, *Living dangerously: Multiculturalism and the politics of difference* (pp. 28–30). New York: Peter Lang Publishing, Inc.

28. Giroux, H. (1993). Democracy. In H. Giroux, *Living dangerously: Multiculturalism and the politics of difference* (pp. 146–148). New York: Peter Lang Publishing, Inc.

29. Giroux, H. (1993). Teachers as cyborgs. In H. Giroux, *Living dangerously: Multiculturalism and the politics of difference* (pp. 137–140). New York: Peter Lang Publishing, Inc.

30. Giroux, H. (1993). Teaching and the new illiteracy. In H. Giroux, *Living dangerously: Multiculturalism and the politics of difference* (pp. 135–137). New York: Peter Lang Publishing, Inc.

31. Giroux, H. (1993). The difficulty of difference. In H. Giroux, *Living dangerously: Multiculturalism and the politics of difference* (pp. 71–74). New York: Peter Lang Publishing, Inc.

32. Giroux, H. (1993). Educational leadership. In H. Giroux, *Living dangerously: Multiculturalism and the politics of difference* (pp. 24–25). New York: Peter Lang Publishing, Inc.

33. Giroux, H. (1993). Pedagogical authority and the politics of the popular. In H. Giroux, *Living dangerously: Multiculturalism and the politics of difference* (pp. 48-49). New York: Peter Lang Publishing, Inc.

34. Giroux, H. (1993). Reclaiming the popular. In H. Giroux, *Living dangerously: Multiculturalism and the politics of difference* (pp. 52-56). New York: Peter Lang Publishing, Inc.

35. Giroux, H. (1993). Toward a pedagogy of representation and representational pedagogy. In H. Giroux, *Living dangerously: Multiculturalism and the politics of difference* (pp. 114-122). New York: Peter Lang Publishing, Inc.

36. Giroux, H. (1991). Introduction: Modernism, postmodernism, and feminism: Rethinking the boundaries of educational discourse. In H. Giroux (Ed.), *Postmodernism, feminism, and cultural politics* (pp. 34-38). Albany: State University of New York Press.

37. Giroux, H. (1996). Introduction: The kids aren't alright. In H. Giroux, *Fugitive cultures: Race, violence, and youth* (pp. 3-12). New York: Routledge.

38. Giroux, H. (1996). Ritualistic, symbolic, and hyper-real violence. In H. Giroux, *Fugitive cultures: Race, violence, and youth* (pp. 60-65). New York: Routledge.

39. Giroux, H. (1996). Cultural pedagogy and children's culture. In H. Giroux, *Fugitive cultures: Race, violence, and youth* (pp. 107-113). New York: Routledge.

40. Giroux, H. (1996). Higher education as a public sphere. In H. Giroux, *Fugitive cultures: Race, violence, and youth* (pp. 120-140). New York: Routledge.

41. Giroux, H. (1996). Cultural work and radio pedagogy. In H. Giroux, *Fugitive cultures: Race, violence, and youth* (pp. 152-161). New York: Routledge.

42. Giroux, H. (1996). The politics of standards. In H. Giroux, *Fugitive cultures: Race, violence, and youth* (pp. 171-174). New York: Routledge.

43. Giroux, H. (1996). Politics and education. In H. Giroux, *Fugitive cultures: Race,

violence, and youth (pp. 177–184). New York: Routledge.

44. Giroux, H. (1997). Intellectual vocations and public celebrities. In H. Giroux, *Channel surfing: Race talk and the destruction of today's youth.* New York: St. Martin's Press.

Teaching Internship

In this chapter we outline the background in our attempt to develop a teacher internship model. We call this model a Reflective and Critical Internship Teaching model (the RCIT model). The model draws upon Giroux's insights on teacher education and reform that is needed to transform universities and faculties of education. We describe this model by using five categories: educational context, key concepts, development of the internship model, critical questions, and classroom management. Finally, in the end of this chapter we present a sample of the cultural work that gets done when seconded teachers, cooperating teachers, university supervisors, and teacher interns engage this RCIT model. We indicate this process by presenting the voices of these stakeholders in the internship process. The voices are clustered around the following issues: the importance of the internship; the value of reflection; identity; dealing with complex issues; praxis and empowerment, and transformation. It is not our attention to describe here the complete process of building this model, as we have done this elsewhere (Kennedy, Doyle, Rose, Singh (1993); Doyle & Kennedy (1995); Singh, Doyle, & Rose (1997); Singh, Doyle, Kennedy, Rose, & Ludlow (2001); Singh (2001)). However, we do describe how we have attempted to incorporate aspects of Giroux's work discussed in the *Reading Giroux*. From our reading of Giroux and others we know that the education reform movements of recent decades in North America forced many institutions to undergo restructuring [Darling-Hammond & Bransford, 2005]. One aspect of this restructuring has been focused on redefining the professional nature of its teaching internship program. In this unfolding context at our institution, we, as a group of education professors, decided to work collaboratively. We saw an opening for a site where we could infuse aspects of reflective and critical pedagogical practice into our teacher education program.

Educational Context

Over the past decade we have developed a model for our work with students, teaching interns, and teachers. We have to be vigorous in claiming that this model was developed, tested, and implemented in conjunction with our colleagues, Andrea Rose and William Kennedy. Our intentions as a team were: to design a collaborative model; to help teaching interns use each other's shared teaching experiences as a medium for reflection; to explore how teaching interns interpret, give meaning to, and make decisions about their experiences at school; to decide what the university team members offer to the teaching interns; to give a framework for assessing reflective thinking; to empower the teaching interns by helping them create their own pedagogical principles; to help teaching interns examine their own beliefs about schools and teaching; and to aid teaching interns in describing and analyzing their own efforts to become reflective. We believe this process represents a model that can be used widely in education. We have also used these pedagogical practices in teacher in-service, as well as at educational conferences, public talks, and seminars in different contexts and sites.

The development of this model draws upon a number of insights provided by Giroux in his massive work in the area of critical theory and pedagogy. Giroux's work is not limited to only these areas. His analyses in connection with democracy, race, gender, class, history, identity, youth, media, modernization, postmodernism, feminism, research, ethics, schooling, education, culture, global economy, politics and various other areas are essential for our teaching purposes. The RCIT Model is designed, in part, to help teachers integrate Giroux's work in a relatively manageable manner for purposes of pedagogical practices. In addition to Giroux's work we have drawn on the writings of many others who use several critical and reflective pedagogical categories to develop teacher education programs. For example, we make use of concepts such as cultural capital, cultural worker, teachers as intellectuals, voice, transformation, problematizing, local theories, reflection, site, difference, culture, ideology, hidden curriculum, social and cultural production and reproduction, and social interaction.

Our own pedagogical practices have been to effect some degree of transformation for the contexts in which we teach. We have focused on the use we make of our authority as teachers to direct this transformation in the creation of conditions that would lead to enhancement of democracy and public spheres. In building the RCIT Model, we have made extensive use of Giroux's writings around the concepts of voice, pedagogical sites, teachers as intellectuals, and troubling of dominant discourses. We have tried to document in our research the extent to which creating safe spaces for students to voice their concerns can lead to some degree of student empowerment and classroom organization. "I am beginning to understand the relationships between the past and how it helps shape our future. New theories and studies help explain how our educational system is shaped by all views that groups and individuals in our society share" (Ken).

Once we realize that teaching interns work and teach out of their own culture, we can also see that cultural production can be theirs. Here, teaching interns can find their voice. It is very easy for interns to be treated as objects. After all they are in a uniquely weak professional role. Once teaching interns come to the realization that their narrative building is liberating, they can grow from that freedom. This freedom building calls for them to go beyond delivery of service to an active critique that examines how they connect with the larger community, culture and society. Teaching interns can use this narrative authorship to "reconstitute their relationship within the wider society" (Giroux, 2005b, p. 153). The language used in reflection, for example, can serve as a means to empower teaching interns to transform their teaching and their lives. This transformation is accomplished over time by building layers of confidence and self-critique.

> I think this kind of reflective process is good for any [one] even for teachers that are teaching for ten years. But this makes it, when you have a meeting with your peers you feel freer to express your opinion because you know people can relate to it. Because, I mean when we had meetings about the discipline and teaching management in our workshops down in our school there were teachers there, some of them were really interested in knowing what others did, so we had that as a main thing. (George)

Because there are so many divergent approaches to teaching we are less interested in changing the intern's perspective than we are in helping the intern be more thoughtful about teaching. In short we wish to help teaching interns become reflective practitioners (Schon, 1983, 1987). We hope to use the praxis of self-reflection, with teaching interns, to help develop a critical reflective stance. Finally we wish to help interns integrate their reflection into everyday praxis and transformation. It is our hope that such critical reflection, in some way, helps rescue teacher education from the limitations of teacher training. We can only work within our own contexts. In this particular university, the RCIT model suggests a person aspiring to a professional practice would have substantive pedagogical knowledge, specific teaching and learning skills, and have developed instructional techniques and would engage in what is generally termed reflective teaching. We have to remember that the reflective practice we represent here is embedded in the praxis of the teaching internship with all its promise and constraints.

Part of our agenda, in this particular pedagogical project, is to give voice to teaching interns as they work at constructing meaning out of their knowledge and experience. Our intention is to help empower interns by using their narratives in a critical fashion that will lead to transformation of their pedagogical thought and action. For this reason it is helpful for us to use the concept of voice as a pedagogical category to examine what possibilities we can share with teaching interns. It is our plan to use a reactive style that consists of eliciting, analyzing, and supporting teaching interns' thoughts and actions. This exercise will allow us to see what teaching interns bring to the school setting as well as to realize the knowledge and culture that students, teaching interns, and teachers can produce among them. Knowledge, and the production of knowledge, can be made less external and more germane to the world of the teaching interns who need to be able to share their understanding of the world with their students. Teaching interns and teachers can collaborate with their students to transform, where necessary, aspects of lived experiences. Transformation, which should be allowed to seep through our institutions and relationships, usually comes in small doses and usually happens over time. Part of being able to be a participant in the ongoing production and creation of culture is the ability for interns to get beyond a practice that may be limited to the reproduction of other people's ideas, values, and beliefs. Our reflective and critical internship program seemed to provide an invaluable site for encouraging and aiding interns' initial exploration of themselves and their practice. Of course there are inherent difficulties and limitations built into the internship experience in terms of interns having to work within the parameters of another teacher's classroom and general school environment. One intern stated, for example, that she did not feel free to be as creative as she would have liked to be and found herself basically reproducing the cooperating teacher's practice. Implied also in her statement is the change that occurred throughout the semester. This intern found ways to explore and develop her own style of teaching. She said, "To a certain degree, at the beginning I was kind of doing what my cooperating teacher did. I wasn't doing what I wanted to do. I felt the need to be more creative" (Jan).

As teacher educators we need to establish a context that rewards reflection on, and critical analysis of, teaching, and that makes transformation possible. What we hope to do is help teaching interns, and ourselves, get beyond the simple accumulation and application of pedagogical principles and methodologies. The process of critical reflection is not easy. It is much easier for us to work in the areas of technical and practical reflection. In this pedagogical project we wish to put emphasis on the experiences, beliefs, sociopolitical values, and goals that underpin interns' thinking. We believe if we can integrate the categories of critical pedagogy, voice, and reflection, we can help in the overall process of teacher education. In particular we want to examine the sources of each teaching intern's knowledge and pedagogical practice. We wish to see teaching interns as human actors and place them at the center of a critical ethnography. We wish to focus on their human agency and explore their local knowledge in the context of their school settings. This will be done in the face of a teacher education logic that puts emphasis on training, skills, and methodologies. We should not treat these categories as non-problematic. We would want, in a dialectical fashion, to place these categories in their social, cultural, and political context. In pedagogical project we wish to explore teaching interns' own learning processes, values, beliefs, and attitudes. How must teaching interns see schooling in a way that allows for the pursuit of a reflective, critical pedagogy? How can teaching interns better appreciate the culture of schools? The day is gone when we can approach the school as if it is simply a place for learning. Schools—the result of complex social, historical and cultural interactions—can no longer operate as if they were gaping monoliths churning out objective information. Schools are living places, in all the complexity that implies. At a very early stage in their professionalism teaching interns are tossed into this tangled web very often with all the voices of dominant educational discourses ringing in their heads. Interns sometimes find themselves faced with conflicting settings. Bert tells of one such situation: "I suggested that we could get the students into smaller groups to work on things, and the teacher said, yes, but we'll put it off for a little while yet and we'll get you used to them in one way" (Bert).

What are some of the concerns that underpin the need for a reflective critical pedagogy? It seems that many of these concerns can be placed in the form of questions. Giroux claims that it is essential for us to question the social and cultural control that is operational in schools and that all educators, including teaching interns, must be aware of the wider social forces at work in schools. Teaching interns can realize that the language, resources, and practices of schools are politically burdened. The challenge is to capitalize on the political nature of schooling so that teaching interns empower themselves to take control of their own growth and transformation. Teaching interns cannot do this until they understand how "human experiences are produced, contested, and legitimated within the dynamics of everyday classroom life" (2005b, p. 133). Teaching interns need to be helped to stand back from their schoolwork and critically examine it through a reflective process. How can teaching interns see schooling as part of a wider process of education? It is important for teaching interns to realize that schooling does not happen within a cultural fortress. How can subjectivity and experience be given a stronger stance within the discourse of schooling? As Giroux and Aronowitz point out there is a tendency to remove both teachers and students from their histories and cultural experiences (1993). This is certainly true for teaching interns. For one thing, they are operating on someone else's work site. They are often expected to follow the mindset and norms evident in that borrowed classroom. Often they inherit a curriculum and methodology designed from a distance for someone else. Product then comes before process, and transmission before transformation. However, it is vital for teaching interns to realize that who is learning precedes what is learned. Here is an opening for teaching interns to treat their students as critical agents and to build on their collective histories and cultures. In other words, teaching interns can help students develop keys to their own transformation. In a real sense we are talking about a reflective model that encourages teacher educators to help empower teaching interns who in turn help empower their students. All of us need to appreciate the power of our knowledge and experience. This might best be realized through structured reflection. Teaching interns need to understand the power built into their own knowledge and to see how that power translates in their interactions with students and administrators. Often teaching interns act as if they are powerless. At other times power is used by teaching interns in ways that can be unknown to them because they have the power of language and culture at their fingertips: a type of hidden curriculum. We all often toss this power around with great abandon. Giroux and Aronowitz claim that strategies need to be developed to identify, invigilate and overcome the patterns of domination built into schooling (1993).

What are the politics of cultural production and reproduction as far as the teacher intern is concerned? Teaching interns, because of the nature of their university course work, often act as if schooling is socially and politically neutral. Clearly there is a fundamental connection between forms selected for transmission within a culture and various forms of domination. Teaching interns need to be able to realize what is hidden in the knowledge they produce and reproduce. We know that education has the power to mystify itself and conceal its power relationships. It is easy to simply follow the curriculum and miss the more subtle messages going out to students.

What are the discrepancies between dominant versions of reality and the lived experience of subordinate groups? Teaching interns need to examine their own teacher view of reality against the real lives of their students. Teaching interns and their students need to accept each other's reality and explore how knowledge can be produced from that acceptance. Schools must be seen as places where both teacher and student grow. This is no less true for teaching interns for they need to understand their situation and appreciate the underlying social structures and power relationships at work within the classroom.

How can teaching interns appreciate the best dimensions of their own histories, experiences, and culture in a fashion that will help them to become transformative intellectuals? Teaching interns, like students generally, are often put in a position where their own histories are treated as incidental and their own experiences as unimportant. This is especially true in a school culture that puts so much emphasis on professional experience. When schooling becomes more instrumental, teaching interns are often removed from their grounding and treated as receivers of dominant discourses on educational attitudes, practices, and methodologies. There is a struggle for teaching interns to hold on to their authentic selves. Still, there is hope.

Teaching interns, we believe, need to be able to speak their minds and share their circumstances in a relatively safe environment. They can likewise examine their own voices as they relive and interrogate their classroom experiences. As teaching interns work through reflection they maneuver between transmission and transformation. They can set out the reality of content and skills as the raw material of transformation. The knowledge and skills can be used as transformative tools for teaching interns to probe their teaching and their own reality.

One of the hardest things for teachers to do is to share the process of learning. All our professional training and thinking is grounded in the assumption that we, as teachers, are supposed to have knowledge; consequently, we are supposed to tell what we know. Unless we work against this instinct to tell, our teaching will remain limited.

> Well, I want to be the type of teacher that doesn't only teach but can learn, to be able to communicate with students in and out of class, because I don't think that what goes on in class is the only important thing. I think what happens outside of class is just as important. I want to be able to engage in conversation with the students, not so much on a personal level but on the factual level. I want them to be able to come to me if they have problems. I want them to know that I'm there, and I also want them to be there for me for support, if I need encouragement about a certain topic or something. I mean students can often do that and they can act as support for you as well and not just [you] for them (Susan).

Yet, the teacher remains essential, and transmitting knowledge remains basic to learning. However, mere telling is not enough. How can we help teaching interns gain that kind of power? How can we encourage teaching interns to build new narratives rather than retell the old stories? If we can put emphasis on building rather than retelling, on producing rather than reproducing, then there is the possibility of a critical pedagogy. We must encourage teaching interns to ask their own questions—questions that extend invitations to reflection. It is important that the teacher educator and the teaching intern reflect together. As indicated earlier, there has been an encouraging growth in reflective practice in teacher education and in professional development.

One of the difficulties we have to guard against when using reflection with teaching interns is that it tends to be what the teacher educator makes it. In other words, the teacher educator's background, interests, and attitudes often become the unintentional focus for a given reflective process. Still, as teacher educators, we have to remind ourselves that it is more important to be aware of the cultural capital of the teaching interns than it is to simply pass on our own world view. If the reflective process is to serve the best interests of the teaching interns, it should examine and build on their cultural capital. It seems necessary to help teaching interns realize the authentic value of their different lifestyles, cultural origins, or belief systems. All of these differences can help make up the reflective mosaic of a critical pedagogy. "We are in a system, where individually you relate to students one on one. After class you talk to them and get to know them. And, you let them know how you are, how you are as a person and they relate to that, too" (Bert).

Henry Giroux tells us that a critical pedagogy must begin with the concrete experiences of everyday life. It seems that critical reflection in the teaching internship can be seen as a "cultural field where knowledge, language, and power intersect" (2005b, p. 133). This intersection can be a place where moral, cultural, and social practices are produced. This is especially true if our intention is simply to give teaching interns voice. Sometimes the giving of voice is much more important than the presentation and the comprehension of new teaching skills or methodologies. As teacher educators we can simply give teaching interns a place to speak their part, a place to use their voices. Teaching interns are able to use their experience, their culture, and their story. This in itself is a real form of power for teaching interns. Out of this power new confidences grow, new social relationships are put in place, and new meanings can be produced.

Part of what teacher educators need to give teaching interns is the understanding that people make their own culture. If teachers and teaching interns begin with trying to tap into the culture of the students rather than confront them with some received culture, then critical pedagogy is already in place. If teachers are dealing with student culture, then the reflection and schoolwork is an extension of that culture. Through such work, teaching interns can work towards self-empowerment and social transformation. Here, particular forms of social knowledge and power relationships can be divested of their oppressive trappings. Teaching interns can build on the cultural material of their own lives, to question, resist, and possibly transform the larger society. Institutional and social transformation is, we believe, achieved in small steps with the assistance of reflective, critical attitudes.

One of the many challenges of a teaching internship is to situate teaching in the wider cultural, social, and political context. This process can be helped by a critical reflection that delves into the practices of schooling from the point of attitude, content, resources, and methodology. Reflection, one of the attributes of critical pedagogy, has several implications for teachers. First, it is essential for students and teachers to leave time for reflection about their school experience. We suggest to the people we work with that reflection be built into the school activity. This is where teacher-student dialogue becomes important. If any school content or experience is treated in a dialectical fashion, questions will naturally follow. Through reflection, teacher educators and teaching interns can learn to examine the relationships between power and knowledge. In this way, they make use of the concept of teaching and learning as a process of inquiry into the problematic. This often represents a large pedagogical leap for both teacher educators and teaching interns; however, it is a leap that we must help each other to take.

For our purposes in this book, a reflective critical pedagogy is seen as one in which teaching interns act as intelligent practitioners who, capable of reflective thought, take responsibility for their own professional development. A reflective, critical pedagogy realizes that education is not a neutral process and that teaching methods cannot be denuded of the social, human and historical elements making up this process. This philosophy is difficult to put into practice. Society expects schools to correct social inequalities and reproduce the given society. Such expectations often leave the beginning teacher intern in the middle of conflicting demands. Often teaching interns feel they have little chance of remedying a situation that is related to complex issues of social class, cultural background, and the institutional biases of social class, cultural background and the institutional biases of schooling. Nonetheless, teaching interns need to be critically aware of these complex issues and realize how teaching fits into the total process. Teaching interns often find themselves faced with conflicting settings.

One of the initial tasks for teaching interns will be to examine the social distance between themselves and their students. They do have roles as educated authority figures. This is not an easy exercise for teaching interns who realize that classroom management is so bound up with social distance. Few teachers or teaching interns would deny that they often use social distance as a means to control classes.

How can teaching interns become involved in both the conception and execution of schoolwork? Teaching interns, like tenured teachers, must ask to do more than simply implement programs designed by others. The notion of separation of concept and execution represents an industrial ideology that does a great disservice to teachers, teaching interns, and students (Giroux & Aronowitz, 1994). Separation of concept and execution makes critical learning improbable. It is not easy for harried teaching interns to resist ready-made learning outcomes along with suggested projects and packaged student questions.

Teaching interns must be given responsibility for their own learning. This assuming of responsibility calls for empowered teaching interns who can control what they do in class and who enable students to reflect and produce their own knowledge. Students should be allowed to explore the contradictions between their schools and the larger society with a view to changing what needs to be changed as well as affirming what needs to be affirmed. Once again this represents a major leap for teaching interns.

Key Concepts

While developing the RCIT model we had a number of key notions in our minds. The conversations about the notion of cultural sites and practice, as presented by Henry Giroux and Roger Simon, have proven to be very useful for our teaching purposes. For example, Simon (1992) explains that a cultural-political site is not an ordinary situation. It is a complex and conflicted location where intricate representational forms are worked out and produced. It is a place where a multiplicity of forces is at work to produce a particular practice. Different things can and do happen at a specific site at a particular time. A site is a place where different possibilities interact. A site is a contested terrain where the specificity of the particular context in which one is located in relationship to others must be taken into account. There could be many sites of production for a particular struggle.

The concepts of teachers as educators, intellectuals, cultural workers, and public intellectuals have been very useful for our pedagogical practices. In the field of education, following Gramsci and others, Giroux (2005b, 1997b) has developed the concept of teachers as intellectuals and cultural workers. Our purpose in this section of the book is to highlight some aspects of this discourse that seem relevant to our pedagogical project. One aspect of our agenda is to describe the meaning of teachers as intellectuals and cultural workers in its strong form and in its moderate form. We do this by way of discussing: (a) the notion of education as a panacea in the historical context of the development of liberal theory of education and society in the North America and other Western countries, and (b) recent educational reform proposals in education. In this way we attempt to study the concept of teachers as intellectuals and cultural workers as articulated by Giroux and Aronowitz (1994) and to clarify implications for our own pedagogical practices. In particular we are interested in developing a pedagogy of affirmation.

As part of our pedagogical practice, we believe in the need to put various bodies of information before our students and teaching interns. One such idea is that education is a panacea for all the ills of the society. This idea has a long history and has been carefully nurtured in liberal education. It is built around the belief that the education system must fulfill many functions in society. Taken in this context, education becomes a major instrument for many social reformers. This tradition is very much alive today (Giroux & Giroux, 2004).

As we work with teaching interns we keep in mind the notions of teachers as intellectuals and cultural workers. We believe that these are very affirming notions. Giroux, in his various writings, asserts that critical and reflective educators should function as public intellectuals at sites that provide them openings and safe spaces for attempting new pedagogical practices. Educators, like other cultural workers such as lawyers, social workers, architects, medical professionals, theologians, and writers, need to rethink and discuss the purpose and meaning of schooling. This should not be taken for granted. Traditionally, artists, writers, and media producers have been seen as cultural workers. Giroux extends the concept and practice of cultural work by including teachers and other educators. In doing so, he is emphasizing the primacy of the political and the pedagogical. Giroux believes that the political dimension of cultural work is crucial. What is at stake, as far as Giroux is concerned, is a political imagery that extends the possibilities for creating new public spheres. In these public spheres the principles of equality, liberty, and justice would become the primary organizing principles. We find that our students do not always appreciate why their pedagogical work should or could extend outside the walls of the classroom. We have found that once teaching interns get a sense of this ideology, they are on their way to becoming intellectuals. If they can make this leap, then they need not be confined to the technical aspects of teaching. It should be noted that we do not belittle the value of information and technology: we simply try to help students keep both in perspective.

Because of the reality of teachers' work in varied sites, we have found it helpful to temper the concept of teacher as intellectual. First of all, for many of the students and teachers we work with, there is an elitist tinge to the term intellectual. Therefore, one of the first tasks we have is to diffuse that word. The introduction of the concepts of strong and moderate intellectual is a beginning for this diffusion. Giroux speaks of two uses of the term teachers as transformative intellectuals. We label these uses as the strong form and the moderate form. In the strong form, teachers as intellectuals are expected to link the political struggle within school to larger social issues, redefine the terrain of politics and citizenship, use their skills to form alliances with various social movements, play the role of social activist, and struggle collectively to transform schools into democratic public spheres. This means that they should be less concerned with embracing professionalism in its narrow sense, securing tenure and promotions, and thinking of schools as institutions whose major function is to serve corporations, or various ideological groups. Instead, teachers as intellectuals, in the strong sense, should defend school as a public service that educates students to become critical citizens. As Giroux encourages us, teachers should feel free to use a language of possibility and hope. Finally, we need to have the courage to denounce social practices that subjugate, violate, and oppress.

When we work with teaching interns and teachers we openly acknowledge the fact that educators work under both ideological and institutional constraints. We cannot expect every educator to be politically active and engage in a wider collective struggle in alliance with various social movements. In other words, it would seem to be unrealistic and unethical to expect every teacher to function in every life situation as a transformative intellectual in the strong sense. Therefore, concrete conditions under which teachers work must be taken into account by those discussing teachers' roles as intellectuals.

We encourage teaching interns to treat their students as persons who have the ability to change their environments, question how knowledge is produced, and engage in dialogue with other students to make knowledge not only meaningful but also critical and emancipatory. This can be achieved, in part, by encouraging students to learn their own history, language, and cultural traditions. Besides engaging in self-confirmation, students are able to question aspects of dominant culture through the process of empowerment.

The Development of the Internship Model

As indicated above, the model we have developed for our work with education students, teaching interns, and cooperating teachers calls for us to introduce new concepts and terms in our courses. Part of this agenda is to help students move back and forth between the micro-and macro-levels of teaching and learning. Giroux is helpful for us here, because he draws upon critical social theory and develops a critical theory of education. Before we can teach about critical theory, we have to build an institutional support structure at our workplace. We have done this by working with colleagues, who can be loosely fitted under the umbrella of critical educators. We develop courses, do research, serve on committees, and hold study sessions. In this way we have established a supportive and safe network of communication among our colleagues. In a sense, we work in self-selecting cohorts. In addition to this, we need to nurture a culture in which undergraduate students and experienced teachers invest their energies in learning about critical perspectives on society, economy, history, politics, and culture. We are aware, from reading Giroux, and our own experience that students are politicized within the dominant conservative and neoliberal ideology of education and are often denied a socialization that is based on critical political education.

In our effort to integrate critical pedagogy into the undergraduate curriculum especially, we have come to be very aware of the difficulties involved in bringing about any sort of quick change. Change has its own logic and it often comes at a slow pace. We have to learn to be patient in attempting to bring about change. Giroux reminds us that there are no easy answers for addressing the major social problems of the time, yet we can contribute to that struggle by attempting to take on the role of a public intellectual. Much of the work we now do is done in a subtle fashion. We have learned that more can be accomplished, over time, by nudging and teasing out than by charging at walls. Resistance can be a quiet process. We will be the first to admit that the patience needed for such a process does not come easy to us. We all have to find our own ways to resistance, hope, and transformation. We are also learning to allow our students to find their own way. Giroux and Aronowitz stress that being an intellectual brings matching responsibility for teachers. As we have claimed above, the role of intellectual is much more than a mantel placed on teachers. This is not a job for which one applies. We stress to the students and teachers we work with, that being an intellectual, in this critical sense, can in fact be a burden. For many teachers it is easier to accept the prepackaged curriculum content and the objectives that are printed in the teacher guides. The role of intellectual for teachers means that this is no longer enough. Now the responsibility is to shape the very purposes and conditions of school. This is where teachers have to take responsibility for their own work. Interns remind us of the constraints that are imposed by the curriculum, as well as by the rules and regulations set by local school administrators. In fact, one of the biggest challenges we face is to convince students that as teachers they can have power. At this crossroads, we encourage students to remember teachers who had power—who gave themselves power. We never try to downplay the difficulty of this. Rather, we prompt these teachers, and would-be teachers, to move quietly but definitely toward such moments. Reminding them that as transformative intellectuals, we never really arrive. We remain in progress. Of course we have to remind ourselves of this also.

In building the RCIT Model, we have taken small steps to encourage our colleagues to cross disciplinary borders in the interest of socializing students within the framework of political education directed towards realizing substantive democracy. One of the key features of the RCIT Model is to encourage students, teaching interns, and teachers to produce "local theories." Local theories are embedded in particular incidents and are seen as describing real situations. It is further asserted that only those who experience those incidents can know the real nature of the situation. The objective discourse is generally perceived as a scientific discourse. In contrast, the discourse of the real maintains that the intuition of experienced teachers and other practitioners is the major force of understanding of classroom situations. This kind of pedagogical work is an empowering practice, according to Giroux and other critical educators. We have been arguing that a support structure needs to be built at the place of work in order to effectively integrate Giroux's versions of critical pedagogy into the curriculum. This is no less true for classroom teachers than it is for those of us who practice pedagogy in faculties of education. In the section that follows, we will comment on the nature of doing reflective and critical collaborative work and describe the process of building alliances with many other groups involved in the process of teacher-education programs at our institution. In particular, we will focus on the teaching-internship aspect of our program.

Practicing a reflective, critical, collaborative pedagogy is a tedious business. Reflection in action is not easy. One assumption in our work has been that reflection is a social process and not simply an individual process. The reality is that prospective teachers, supervisors, cooperative teachers and administrators located in the institution and the schools are all active learners. In developing a model for working in the teaching internship as part of a larger teacher-education program, we self-consciously asked what supervisors bring to the teaching internship. We want to stress that although we can and often do, reflect-in-action, it is seldom that we make this reflection public. It might be of value, in mapping out our pedagogical project, to indicate how we come together as a team. As we have stressed earlier, the RCIT Model was developed, over time, by four of us working in close collaboration. How did we establish such an internal collaboration? How did the four of us, representing different disciplines, come to work together? Reflecting on, and coming to grips with, such issues as who will collect the data, write the narrative, judge the work, present the findings, as well as what sort of data will be collected and how it will be analyzed, are necessary in establishing internal collaboration. Since all of these issues involve taking action, they can be seen as important events in establishing collaboration. Before we could even think about working with students or teachers we had our own work to do. Events take place at a particular time, in a given space and under certain conditions; it was no different for us as we developed, with our colleagues, this RCIT model for working with teaching interns.

We work in a relatively large institution at a major university in Canada. We indicated above that we have suffered from the logic and practice of downsizing. Structurally, formerly independent departments were moved into one large unit. The new expectation was that faculty members would freely interact with each other, and at least to some degree, cross the discipline boundaries and previously entrenched departmental orientations. These institutional adjustments brought changes in the organization of the teacher-education program as a whole and of the teaching-internship program in particular. In this context several faculty members explored the possibility of regrouping themselves with other colleagues. This new setting facilitated bringing our group together to work collaboratively on the teaching-internship program in the institution. However, this attraction to work together was not totally circumstantial. Based on our previous work (Doyle, 1993: Singh, Hamnett, Porter & Kumar, 1984) in critical studies we discovered that we were, in certain aspects, sympathetically predisposed to each other's orientation to education, schooling, and society. All these factors encouraged us to work together.

We realized from the beginning that it would be unrealistic to think that our work could be carried out in any meaningful way without the help of others. We needed external collaboration. We expected cooperating teachers, seconded teachers working as supervisors, principals and vice-principals, secretaries and other staff members in schools, and our colleagues in the faculty, whose responsibility it was to run the teaching-internship program, to play key roles in the organization and successful completion of our project. We never underestimated the fact that each category of people would bring its own cultural capital to this teaching-internship program. These people were the individuals who had regular contact with the routines and rhythms of schools, students, and teachers. They had first-hand experience of observing students' behaviors in real situations in the classrooms. These others, especially the cooperating teachers and the seconded teachers who worked as university supervisors, knew the contexts, sites, situations, and practices of many schools in the province. Persuaded by the fact that these groups of people had much to offer to us about the culture of schools, we began by contacting them. Our own orientation was to listen sympathetically to others, talk with them, understand what they had to say, and learn from their experiences. We realized that respecting others' local theorizing and genuinely trusting their insights about the complex nature of schooling were the key factors in establishing good communication and working relationships.

How did we go about doing this? We went to orientation seminars organized by our colleagues who were responsible for the delivery of the teaching-internship program in the faculty. There we met the cooperating teachers, seconded teachers, teaching interns, and representatives of school boards and the Department of Education. We listened to the voices of different individuals, recognizing the importance of those voices, and accepting the fact that they did operate both at the macro-and micro-levels of the school environment. These seminars we considered as sites for reflection-in-action. We observed those who could speak with authority and those who had to listen. In addition, we saw how the participants went about empowering each other and how they were able to clarify their own authority without silencing others. In these orientation seminars we observed how an attempt was made to create an enabling teaching-internship culture based on an authentic attempt to create safe spaces for participants to express their feelings, emotions, and sentiments. It became obvious to us that working objectively with others did not mean ignoring human feelings. We learned that engaging with others, in order to do collaborative work, meant first of all, learning to trust and respect others. In education, social working relationships are built more on trust and respect and less on authority. We learned also that creating sites for others, where they could take ownership of their own affairs, not only reduces dependence and enhances creativity but also empowers others by encouraging them to desire more and attain their wishes. We learned that engaging with others meant accepting differences. Our goal was to aid people to work in their own ways and within their own contexts. We were trying to practice what we were reading. We were attempting to put Giroux's writings into practice.

Part of the need, in order to develop a reflective and critical model of teacher education, was to sensitize ourselves about how others analyzed dominant practices and discourses in the area of teacher education, and the teaching internship in particular. We viewed this as a part of a larger issue relating to teacher education in North America and elsewhere, especially in the context of increasing globalization of economy and culture. We learned how others tried to be reflective through the process of questioning, and compared their ways of probing and seeing things with our own. This was one way we attempted to add a critical aspect to the teaching internship building process.

Giroux claims that it is crucial for us to challenge and redefine the borders of our pedagogies. It is essential to create pedagogical conditions in which students also become border crossers. In this way they can better understand otherness on its own terms. It can be said that our understanding of otherness and difference are essential to any critical pedagogy.

Another way we attempted to make this program critical was to function as cultural workers. In seeing things differently in many areas, at the discussions with our collaborators, we were also functioning as critical educators. We tried to insert into the ongoing conversations our own concerns about the difference between teacher education and teacher training. We saw the teaching-internship program as a site not only for learning classroom-management techniques, although we fully realized the fact that these techniques formed the overriding concern of many teaching interns and seconded teachers. We asserted that pedagogy was a form of cultural and political production rather than simply a transmission of knowledge and skills. Part of our intention was to share with others our understanding of pedagogy. We wanted to share how pedagogy helped all of us recognize our own relationships with each other and our environment. How could we establish working, collaborative relationships with all those involved in teacher education in this province? How could we understand the relationship between schooling, education, and the dynamics of social power? How could we understand what we say and do? How else could we understand what we agree to exclude or include? How could we accept the authority of some experts and deny others? How could we accept privileging of one form of vision about the future over the other? We constantly went back to reading Giroux, as we worked our way through this process. As we have said before, we believe that transformation is done over time, in quiet ways.

Our discussions with teachers and teaching interns were filled with local theorizing on various aspects of the complex nature of schooling and classrooms. "I think reflective skills are important. However, we need to have a knowledge base on which to reflect. In schools, students should be guided to learn and think for themselves" (Peter). Learning to conceptualize one's own everyday life experiences in one's own voice is a step toward becoming a reflective and critical person. Recognizing that one has the ability, the linguistic resources, and above all, the courage and confidence to theorize is another step in opening windows of possibility.

> It is clear that we're all having trouble understanding what the authors of the various articles are saying. However, I think this is a positive thing because we are learning and helping each other understand the issues. As well, we're questioning and analyzing the ideas presented. We're not taking them at face value but rather, we are critically examining the articles that is, I think, the most important thing, or one of the most important things that we can learn to do as future teachers (Veronica).

The transcriptions of our discussions, some of which we are sharing here, revealed to us that we were successful in creating safe spaces for the participants who were then able to create a language of possibility. This form of practice enabled participants to create sites where they could imagine the possibility of achieving their desires and fulfilling their wishes. The seconded teachers, for example, saw this reflective and critical teaching internship program as a site where they could genuinely contribute to the advancement of teacher education in this province. "I think the internship program is definitely one of the most important things that students do in becoming teachers" (Judy). This was an empowering moment for them. These experienced teachers could see their roles and visualize structural changes that could be brought about in the existing educational system that could build bridges between teachers in schools and professors at the institution. This bridging could lead to the stronger linking of theory and practice. In many ways these educators were now open to a discourse that they never had before.

In time we added the reflective and critical aspect of our pedagogical project in ongoing conversations with the teaching interns, who were now working in various school classrooms. There, as part of our routine work, we engaged ourselves as supervisors and attempted to create what we term the mini-reflective sites within the school settings. As is the general practice, we made extensive notes in the classroom and gave feedback about how we saw interns in action. The purpose was to encourage interns to analyze their teaching and reflect on their ways of knowing. This did not mean that we were timid in using our own authority as supervisors and exposing teaching interns to professional knowledge. Obviously, part of our intention was to share knowledge, but we were continuously reflecting-in-action and simultaneously examining our own knowledge. How else could we encourage them to take ownership of their teaching internship? We created these mini-reflective sites in the school settings to help them achieve this goal.

We also involved the cooperating teachers in these mini-reflective sites. Inviting the cooperating teachers to share extensive notes on teaching interns, we opened ourselves to the critique of the practicing cooperating teachers.

This we did to find out what the practicing classroom teachers bring to the teaching internship. In our orientation seminars and in reading the literature in the area of teacher education, we heard repeatedly that university-based supervisors often have little knowledge of real classroom situations and that what they have to offer as advice is often too theoretical. "I'm going to say that in my view the active teacher who is seconded to be a supervisor might have the edge over the university professor who hasn't been in the classroom situation for some time" (Patricia). Thus, opening ourselves to the critique of cooperating teachers was a learning experience. We compared and contrasted our notes, recognizing and respecting each other's situational authority at different levels of the schooling process. The teaching interns and their cooperating teachers also compared and contrasted their notes separately. Then, at the mini-reflective sites, we entered into the reflection process. Our intention was to accord recognition to the different voices, privileging each of them in their own authentic ways. We always reminded ourselves that reflection was a social process and that all parties involved in it learn from each other.

Besides creating the mini-reflective sites in the school settings, we created another site for reflection at the institution. We saw these reflective sessions as safe sites away from school routines. After talking to each other, we decided to work with a larger party of teaching interns, so we combined our smaller groups. The main purpose for using this larger group was to create a site and opportunity where the teaching interns could voice their experiences of the teaching internship, reflect together on those experiences, and also share their experiences with others at different levels of reflectiveness. We conceptualized the reflective session as being a site where the teaching interns would be enabled to practice reflection-in-action. These reflective sessions have become a somewhat regular feature of the teaching internship program in the faculty.

We could not have developed these reflective sessions as sites for transformation without the input of many of our colleagues, who are in charge of delivering and administering the teaching-internship program in the faculty and who themselves have extensive experience in the area of teacher education. This is where the faculty solidarity building, we talked about above, came into play. Similarly, we discussed with several cooperating teachers, principals, and vice-principals the idea of building a reflective and critical teaching internship program. In scheduling all of these reflective sessions, we consulted with the cooperating teachers and the teaching interns. The intention was to avoid disrupting the schedule of the school and rhythms of the cooperating teachers and the teaching interns. We kept each party informed of the process and elicited their feedback on the idea of conducting reflective sessions as a part of the teaching internship program. It became clear to us that in order for us to organize these sessions, the collaboration of all parties was essential.

Critical Questions

There are many questions that call for the fuller development of a reflective critical pedagogy. In interpreting and adapting the work of Giroux we raised the following sets of questions:

In striving for authenticity, how do we as educators stand back from our own teaching and move beyond the mere execution of classroom skills and the delivery of discipline content? If individual experience is negated, is it possible that the individual is silenced? Can teaching interns be empowered to speak around these silences? Can teaching interns be given authorship of their own work and life stories? Can they develop a language of possibility that works against inherited dominant discourses? How can we help teaching interns gain power so that they are able to function as teachers who challenge, arouse interests, instill confidence, coordinate achievement and encourage reflection? How can we encourage teaching interns to build new narratives rather than retell old narratives? How can teachers who keep their own stories hidden expect students to value each other's stories? How does the teaching intern relate to the wider experiences of the school? Does the teaching intern appreciate the values, beliefs, and attitudes at work in the given community? How does the school reflect the economic, political, and cultural aspects of the society? How can teaching interns get beyond the limitations and grind of everyday school life? How must teaching interns see schooling in a way that allows for the pursuit of a reflective critical pedagogy? How can teaching interns better appreciate that the culture of schooling is not simply a single, unified set of patterns? How can teaching interns realize their potential as agents for transformation? What are some of the concerns that underpin the need for a reflective, critical pedagogy? How can teaching interns see schooling as part of a wider process of education? How can subjectivity and experience be given a stronger stance in schooling? What histories are in place before any learning is attempted? What are the politics of cultural production and reproduction as far as the teacher intern is concerned? What are the discrepancies between dominant versions of reality and the lived experience of subordinate groups? How can teaching interns help break down some of the real barriers to transformative teaching and learning by opening fresh ways of going about the process of schooling? How can teaching interns learn to see and examine the ideology behind knowledge and culture? How do teaching interns produce a critical dialogue that will aid in their own empowerment? How can teaching interns become involved in both the conception and execution of schoolwork? How can teaching interns appreciate the best dimensions of their own histories, experiences, and culture in a fashion that will help them to become transformative intellectuals?

We believe that it is essential for us to affirm the voices of hope. What does it mean to be a reflective and transformative intellectual? Can we voice our hope in the midst of many political, economic and cultural difficulties we face today in the field of education? Can we insist on the possibility of collectively constructing a viable reflective teaching-internship program? What are the necessary conditions for educating teaching interns to be intellectual or cultural workers? How do other people participate in particular ways of life in schools? How are these ways of life produced and challenged? What forms of local theorizing are being done? What forms of knowledge do school cultures in this province legitimize and what forms do they disdain? What is the place of studying privileged discourses in education in the process of building a Reflective and Critical Internship Teaching Model? In what ways is it possible for teaching interns to function as intellectuals and cultural workers?

We also have to examine the significance of cultural capital and traditions in relation to teacher education. Is there a cultural capital unique to teacher education? In order to be successful in a teaching internship program is it necessary to acquire a new cultural capital? Do we prepare teaching interns to perpetuate isolation from cultural traditions or do we encourage and prepare them to take into account the lived cultures of students? Are there possibilities within the teacher education program for negotiation in the production of knowledge, values, beliefs, and meanings? Is there room to contest and resist or do teaching interns perceive their situations to be unalterable? Are teaching interns empowered and equipped to be agents of production and transformation?

The RCIT Model

In many ways we are involved with the experience of reflective practice (Figure 1). We have to remember that the reflective practice we refer to is embedded in the praxis of the teaching internship with all its promises and constraints. It is not easy for those of us involved in this teacher-education program to exam-

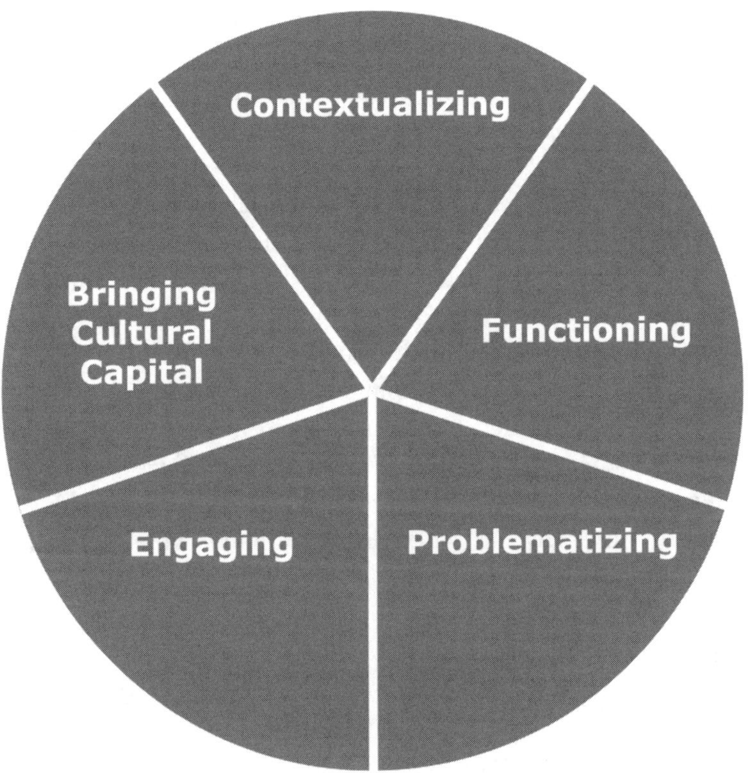

Figure 1 - RCIT Model

ine our living in a critical sense because we take so much for granted. It is hard to uncover the nature of the forces that inhibit and constrain our actions. But if we want to commit ourselves to changing those conditions, then there are, we believe, certain forms of actions we need to pursue with respect to our building up a reflective teacher-education program. In the section that follows we will outline these forms of action we have followed and some of their elements. They correspond to a series of questions we are using while building up the teaching internship program. In this pedagogy of affirmation we have used five forms of action: a) describing and contextualizing, b) bringing and recognizing cultural capital, c) engaging in communication, d) examining and problematizing dominant practices and discourses, and e) functioning as intellectuals and cultural workers.

In this particular model for working with teaching interns we put emphasis on describing and contextualizing. We encourage interns to ask what is the context, case, situation, or practice? What are the sites and institutions? Who are the people involved and what are their actions? What knowledge of reality shapes our interaction? What significant issues are involved? How do these questions include the elements of whom, what, and when?

We examine what cultural capital is brought to the teaching and learning situation. What theories, ideologies, practices, stereotypes, prejudices, and taken-for-granted realities do different partners bring to the teaching internship? What do university supervisors bring to the teaching internship? What do cooperating teachers bring to the teaching internship? What do teaching interns bring to the teaching internship? What does the larger teacher-education program offer to the teaching internship?

Communication in the teaching internship program is crucial. How would we inform ourselves about the complexity of engagement? How do we recognize different voices? How do we reflect about the political and social nature of schooling? How do we see classroom actions that contribute to personal and social change? How do we encourage and empower all the members involved in the teaching internship so that they can engage each other in purposeful communication? Where do we look for windows or openings for reflection-in-action? How do we prepare sites or create new sites for reflection-in-action? When and where do we infuse ideas and actions during conversations with others? What are the risks of making one's own intentions public in the reflection process? What can be gained from such sharing? What is the best way to clarify one's own authority, avoid silencing others, and create safe spaces for others' voices? How can we enable others to disclose their feelings, attitudes, fears and hopes? How can we practice the art of connecting social (macro) and personal (micro) levels of issues? In other words, how can we as university supervisors indulge in the sociological imagination?

One of the biggest challenges is in problematizing dominant practices and discourses. We have to ask what practices are taken for granted in schools? What are habitual ways of talking about ideas and practices during personal, professional and official conversations? Do we need to be listening for what is not being said? Should we cast doubts on what is being said through questioning? Do we share our feeling of uncertainty about institutional regulations? Are we being aware that the social reality of school practice, theories, concepts, and policies is often created through using language in selected ways? Should we share our understanding of how the social history of various theories, concepts, and practices came into vogue?

In the quest to function as intellectuals and cultural workers we can ask how might I transform my own work? How might I do things differently? How do I remind myself of the difference between educator and trainer? Do I see pedagogy as a form of cultural and political production rather than simply involving the practices of knowledge and the transmission of skills? Do I understand how pedagogy helps people to recognize their own relationships with others and the environment that surrounds them? Do I understand that pedagogy helps people to create and organize knowledge, desires, values and social practices? How do I best share an understanding of the relationship of schooling, pedagogy, and cultural practices to the dynamics of social power? Do I have the courage and hope to find ways to effect democratic changes? How can the work we do in a reflective teaching internship help local theorizing? How can we aid the production of knowledge and expand the language of possibility?

Classroom Management

The notion of classroom management, and its narrower reference, discipline, is so significant that in many ways it becomes the indicator of teacher quality. Even the shortest conversation about a given teacher soon centers on his or her ability to manage a classroom. In fact in its most simplistic expression good teaching has become synonymous with good discipline. Any casual discussion about teaching and students invariably turns to terms like control, behavior, noise, trouble, quiet, or respectful. In fact one of the most frustrating things that can be said to a teacher is that "your class is so noisy." Few teachers will respond with a "thank you, they are learning." There is no intent here to claim that classroom management and discipline are not important. Yet, classroom management is not teaching. Classroom management is a necessary condition for teaching. Therefore claiming that because there is no noise in a classroom, and students sit in rigid rows and raise their hands before speaking means that effective teaching is happening is not well founded. Teaching and learning are much too complicated acts for that.

We can also remind ourselves that there are many kinds of learning; hence we need different methods of teaching. It follows that there are many aspects to classroom management. In some ways we can think about models of classroom management that allow us to set goals and objectives, shape curriculum, design instructional materials, and guide instruction and evaluation. We can see classroom management not only as a precondition for teaching and learning but as an integral part of the whole process. In a practical sense experienced teachers do not shift gears from classroom management to instruction in a structured way. However, a necessary understanding about teaching and classroom management as well as helpful skills need to be in place. Effective teaching and management skills must be grounded in solid thinking. If the grounding thinking is not present the laundry list of skills will run out sooner or later. There is a real trap in the demand from inexperienced teachers to "tell me how to do it." The trap is that the "how to" formulas often leave teachers frustrated in the face of new demands and circumstances. These formulas need to be tempered with "why am I doing this" question. There is no facile attempt here to say that it is all so easy and claim, "that all you have to do is follow my lead."

We can have teaching without learning and we can have learning without teaching, and we certainly can have classrooms managed without any of the above happening. There is the expressed assumption that teachers' behavior can influence student learning! The challenge is to reach out to different students and create a multidimensional educational environment. As any professional teacher will tell you, this is not easy.

In the comments above there is much emphasis on the fact that teaching is a complex process that involves decision making and structured reflection. Classroom management, like teaching itself, can be seen as a decision-making process. In order to be effective classroom-management decision makers we need to have competence in: the theoretical knowledge about classroom management; the attitudes that foster effective classroom management; as well as a repertoire of classroom-management skills. In addition to this we need to be reflective educators. That is we need to think about: how research findings may help our practice; select strategies and resources that work well in our particular teaching context; and use our past experience and apply new understandings to immediate classroom-management concerns.

The impetus to include classroom management as a key site in building the RCIT model came from our desire to address the practical needs of our teaching interns. These interns are fearful of management and discipline problems which they anticipate facing in today's complex classroom situations. The voices of John, Susan and Mary represent the concerns of many teacher interns in this regard: "There are students who don't always pay attention and I'm not totally confident in my ability to keep things under control" (John). "Well, one of my biggest worries was discipline. Like if I could keep them under control" (Susan). "My biggest fear, I would say, was maintaining control of the classroom and getting up there and actually having them listen to me" (Mary).

To counter some of the concerns that we hear we have asked ourselves the following questions: What can teacher-internship programs, cooperating teachers and internship supervisors do to enable teacher interns to feel confident in managing classrooms during their internship semester in schools? What can the teacher interns do to empower themselves so as to (a) produce their own strategies and "philosophies" of discipline and education, (b) manage classroom problems, and (c) overcome fear related to discipline and control in classrooms? What are the various strategies suggested by researchers that teacher interns might use for effective classroom management?

Teacher interns are involved in problematizing their everyday experiences. We noted earlier that they struggle, individually and collectively, with dominant discourses in many areas such as classroom management, instruction, resources, discipline, the ability level of students, the purpose of the internship program, the culture of school life and many other such matters. Our focus here is on the fear the teacher interns had about classroom management. At various reflective sites we were able to encourage teacher interns to voice their concerns about classroom management with us, as their supervisors. We were also able to make these reflective sites safe enough for them to share their stories with the other teacher interns. Below we provide a sample of teacher interns' voices that illustrate their concerns and fears about classroom management/discipline/control during the internship program. "There are students who don't always pay attention and I'm not totally confident in my ability to keep things under control" (Joyce). "And you're going to encounter discipline problems. This is what I expected and that's exactly what I saw. I had no illusions, really, that were shattered by this internship experience" (Morgan).

Typically, teaching interns voiced their concerns about the junior high students in a fearful manner. They often thought children in grades seven, eight and nine created more classroom management problems and dealing with them was the worst experience. The concern of one intern provides a clear representation of the views of a substantial number of teaching interns: "My first fear was that I would be put in a junior high school where I would be teaching a wide variety of subjects, many of which I have very little idea about, and to have to face the discipline problems" (Jeff). The teaching interns lamented that they were not adequately prepared at the university to deal with problems related to classroom management. Consequently, they felt they had to look somewhere else for help. Frequently, they thought of seeking help from their cooperating teachers or from other experts who conducted seminars, conferences and workshop on the topic of classroom management. The teaching interns voiced their concern about the lack of preparation at the university in the following typical ways: "That's I think one thing you have to learn in this internship. I think university is, like I said, too idealistic, to many theories and you just got to come back to the practical" (Jayna). They also expressed their dependence on cooperating teachers to learn about classroom management in the following typical voices: "My cooperating teacher sometimes came down on me. I know I have to come up with different ways to control the class and to exert discipline, not in the negative sense of the word but in a positive sense" (Scott).

The interns were most interested in learning the techniques of classroom management from other teachers in their respective schools. They also thought that the internship program offered them a unique opportunity to learn about classroom management techniques. Typically, they voiced their concern about how to sharpen their skills to control the children in the classroom in the following way: "Oh, well, you have to learn a number of classroom management skills. You have to learn how to handle certain situations with individual students that may be disruptive or may not be working to your particular teaching strategy" (Maria).

At various reflective sites we encouraged the teacher interns to reflect on the issues related to classroom management. It was through self-reflection that the teaching interns grappled and struggled to make sense of their actions in regards to classroom management. The following voices of interns illustrate the struggle:

> I used to take the student behavior personally and if someone was doing too much talking and wouldn't listen to me, then I took that personally. And I had to learn to separate my anger from, you know, from. Well, I had to stop being angry. You know what I mean? And I had to. if I was to appear angry, then I, you know. I had to learn to appear angry without being angry, put that face and. I found that a little bit tough to do. And there were times when I became frustrated with. with the class if they weren't getting what I was saying. And so, I don't know if I would classify myself as angry in that situation, but I had to deal with the frustration and be calm and. and not. you know, have patience. (Morley)

Finally it is through a combination of reflection and production of 'local theories' that the teaching interns empowered themselves. Through voicing their concerns in the form of local theories interns developed creative and reflective power. In this way the interns were able to connect their own experiences to classroom management and capitalize on their own cultural capital. They were also able to go back to their own stories, reflect on each other's techniques of control and discipline in classrooms, and produce their own ways of seeing classroom management. In this way, they could produce their own techniques of classroom management. Local theorizing and reflection also seemed to help the interns to connect their own language and lived experiences in classrooms at various sites created for reflection. At these sites we were not interested in negating the individual's experiences and thus silencing them. Our purpose was to create an environment where the interns could feel free to speak out their experiences and thus have a voice. Through reflection and local theorizing, using their own material for story telling, the interns were able to take over the authorship and ownership for producing their own classroom management techniques. They were able to practice reflection-in-action and thus produce their own classroom culture conducive to classroom management to some degree of success.

> I know for next class already that I think I'll, I will be a little less anxious because it was my first class. I'll slow down and I will write neater on the board, so there's something I've learned already. I will try to interact more, I think, ask them more questions, because the one thing I've learned already about classroom management is that you never assume that they know everything. I mean it may seem simple to you or

I, but my God, simple words may just blow them away. You know, simple concepts will blow them away. (Zac)

In building the Reflective and Critical Internship Teaching Model (The RCIT model), we assumed the challenge was how could the cooperating teachers and supervisors structure the teaching interns' voices and produce an internship experience that reflected and built on interns' voices. We reasoned if interns could have sites for reflection and for producing 'local theories' about classroom management, they might be able to speak to their own classroom realities with more confidence. They could self-consciously reflect on their own construction of classroom reality, their own transformation. By this we did not mean that the cooperating teachers and the university based supervisors let the interns do what they liked and pleased. That would not be responsible and would be a great disservice done to a form of teacher education that aspires to be reflective, critical and transformative. So we did actively structure their experience to some extent and hoped to transform interns' concerns about classroom management through engaging them in critical practices such as reflection, problematizing, voicing and local theorizing. We read in their voice that some transformation did take place in their outlook on classroom management. But in structuring their responses we were always cognizant of our earlier advice that this transformation is accomplished over time by building layers of confidence and self-critiques" (Doyle, 1993, p. 132). The critical and reflective experience we are sharing as a group begins the process encouraging interns beyond the mere acquisition of technical skills toward a place where they can feel safe to put their own work into a wider social, cultural, and political context.

Engaging the RCIT Model

Part of our overt agenda from the beginning has been to give voice to the teaching interns with whom we work. At this point it is helpful to hear the voices of interns. Listening to the voices of teacher interns and cooperating teachers will give us some idea about what sort of cultural work gets produced when we are engaged with the RCIT model. The following sections offer a small sampling of their voiced reflection. The names we use are fictitious. For the purposes of this section we address the following issues: the importance of the internship; the value of reflective sessions; creating one's own teacher identity; being aware of complex issues; transformation, and finally we present the voices of seconded teachers.

The Importance of the Internship
In relation to the development of praxis in teacher education, many interns indicated awareness that the internship experience was a crucial step in connecting theory and practice. One intern indicated, for example, that not all theories and practices would be appropriate or relevant for all individuals and situations. Implied in his statement is the need for open-mindedness, flexibility, and adaptability in the development of praxis: "It [internship] couldn't have come at a better time. It was a chance to see theory in practice. Sometimes the theory is true, and sometimes you see the theory is not true at all" (George).

The Value of Reflective Sessions
One of the many challenges of an internship is to situate teaching in the wider cultural, social, and political context. This process can be helped by critical reflection that delves into the practices of schooling from the viewpoints of attitude, content, resources, and methodology. Reflection, one of the attributes of critical pedagogy, has several implications for teaching interns. First, it is essential for students and teachers to leave time for reflection about their school experience. An intern in one group discussion echoed the need for such reflection.

> This is like a process of brainstorming. Like doing something in class and going home and writing about it; reflecting on it yourself, well that's great, that's one thing. But it's not the same as hearing everyone else reflect on it. And I really can't see - having survived a lot of things - like you said, things that have worked and I've tried. You said things that haven't worked and then I've known maybe a suggestion of how to get through them. So I think this is excellent and I really feel bad for students that didn't take part. (Mark)

A member from another group claimed:

> I think this kind of reflective process is good for any [one], even for teachers that are teaching for ten years. But this makes it, when you have a meeting with your peers you feel more free to stress your opinion because you know people can relate to it. Because, I mean when we had meetings about the discipline and teaching management in our workshops down in our school, there were teachers there, some of them were really interested in knowing what others did, so we had that as a main thing. (Melanie)

Some interns expressed remarkably positive reactions to being involved with experiences that provided opportunity for communication. Concerning these reflective seminars, one intern stated:

> I found the seminars to be really helpful. If I didn't have those, I would not have thought about things too much. Even trying to get my thoughts together before the seminars was really helpful. The questions that other people came up with and the differing points of view broadened my own point of view. I find that if I just write [journal] it doesn't help that much. It's better for me if I can talk about it to someone and sometimes even better if they disagree so I can get a wider view on it. (Hank)

Regarding the reflective group seminars, this intern stressed that:

> Overall, I found the seminars facilitated the internship 100%. You get to see other people's opinions. And I've tried them, and they worked. I don't know how other people feel about this, reflecting in your journal. Now I'm terrible at this. I find it really difficult, and I find this [reflective] process here is much better for me personally, maybe this is kind of personal . . . you have something else and you still discuss and reflect. So for me personally I find this really helpful. If I only had the journal, it wouldn't have been half as effective. (Maria)

With regard to the reflective and interactive journal writing, another intern discussed his own use of the journal as a means of basic organization and as a means for critical examination, analysis, reflection, and problem solving:

> It [journal writing] really helped. It's not until you have to articulate something or write it down that you have to clear your thoughts. And nothing forces you to organize your thoughts more than having to write them on paper, day to day, over a month or a semester. It's a way to look at problems, ideas, and other areas to work out. (Jerry)

Creating One's Own Teacher Identity

Part of the joy of being able to be a participant in the ongoing production and creation of culture is seeing the ability of interns to get beyond a practice that may be limited to the reproduction of other people's ideas, values, and beliefs. Our reflective and critical internship program seemed to provide an invaluable site for encouraging and aiding interns' initial exploration of themselves and their practice. Of course there are inherent difficulties and limitations built into the internship experience in terms of interns having to work within the parameters of another teacher's classroom and general school environment. One intern stated, for example, that she did not feel free to be as creative as she would have liked to be and found herself basically reproducing the cooperating teacher's practice. Implied also in her statement is the change that occurred throughout the semester. This intern found ways to explore and develop her own style of teaching. She said: "To a certain degree, at the beginning, I was kind of doing what my cooperating teacher did. I wasn't doing what I wanted to do. I felt the need to be more creative" (Jan).

Another intern indicated awareness that her cooperating teacher had developed a successful teaching style that was unique to her goals, philosophy, and personality. The intern acknowledged also that her own practice would have to be a different one; that is, one built upon her own personal and professional skills and knowledge: "I found my cooperating teacher a bit intimidating. For what she does and the way she thinks, she does an excellent job. Even if your way is different" (Sandra).

Being Aware of Complex Issues

Society expects schools to correct social inequalities and reproduce the given society. Such expectations often leave the beginning teacher intern in the middle of conflicting demands. Often interns feel they have little chance of remedying a situation that is related to complex issues of social class, cultural background, and the institutional biases of schooling. Nonetheless, interns are often critically aware of these complex issues and realize how teaching fits into the total process. Interns sometimes find themselves faced with conflicting settings. Bert tells of one such situation:

> I suggested one time that we could get the students into smaller groups to work on things, and the teacher said, yes, we could do that, but we'll put it off for a little while yet and we'll get you used to them in one way. I kind of want to get into as many methods as I can of teaching. (Bert)

The following comments from three interns make the point that they are learning from their own work: "A good teacher is not only well-prepared but understands the individual student and sees [him/her] as a fellow human being. She lets everyone feel some degree of success" (Denis). "I want them to say they learned from me and me from them . . . and they will remember being here with me. In a way it's scary, but I want to have a positive influence on them and their future" (Joan).

> Yes, I have grown. Through interaction with others I found myself with more confidence. I look at students differently, with a little more compassion. That is good for them and me. I have found through interaction that I do care very deeply. I found myself wondering why students were or were not doing so well at midnight. So I think I have benefited from them more than they have from this experience. (John)

Transformation
Toward the development of productive and transformative practice, some interns expressed understanding concerning the importance of getting beyond the notion of reproductive teaching; that is, merely passing on knowledge or transmitting it to students. This teaching intern demonstrated an awareness of the importance of the human agency in the teaching/learning process: "I hope that I have an interest in people, more so probably than in just teaching to pass on information" (Sandra).

Another intern expressed an understanding that teachers play an active and important role in the preparation of students for life experiences. Implied in his comment is the need for a teaching/learning process that nurtures those individuals equipped with skills necessary for lifelong learning and active participation in culture and society:

> I see teaching as being the most important job in society today. You teach them [students] and you have to prepare them for life no matter what they are going to be. You get a chance to make a difference. I think you can really make a difference. (Hank)

We discovered within the education system evidence of some general understanding concerning the nature of negotiation, as well as of the production of one's own knowledge, values, and traditions. One statement made in a written journal entry at the end of the internship program indicates the development of a language of possibility for this intern, as well as recognition of the need for ongoing critical examination, reflection, and analysis in the processes of decision making and problem solving. This intern's indication of readiness for dealing with the issues of resistance and change may well lead to a productive and transformative practice. She stated: "As I look forward to working in my own school, I hope that I can make certain changes that I feel need to be made, and that these changes are positive for everyone. I hope I never maintain or accept the status quo if I feel it is unacceptable" (Judy).

The Voices of the Seconded Teachers
In this section we describe the results of our collaborations with seconded teachers. These are experienced teachers who have been hired by the university for a period of time to work with interns. In our reflective sessions with seconded teachers we focused primarily on listening to their assessment of the unfolding nature of teacher education generally and the teacher-internship program in particular.

It is clear from our conversations that supervising teachers and cooperating teachers perceive the internship experience to be a significant element in the professional and personal development of all parties involved in teacher education. Here are some typical statements:

> I think it's invaluable to any intern to get some practical experience before they launch off on their own careers on their own. Because they do develop some idea of what it takes to plan and I mean what it takes to deal with classroom management, what it takes to deliver a lesson, what it takes to evaluate homework and to evaluate exams and so on. This is all practical experience and the advantage of doing it through an internship is that if they make mistakes there's two or three people available to help bail them out. There's the cooperating teacher and there's the university supervisor. (Dorothy)

Generally, these experienced teachers recognize their contribution to the continuing development of the internship program. For example, this seconded teacher said:

> Well, I think the internship program is definitely one of the most important things that students do in becoming teachers. I worked on this last year with six teachers and at that time, we did really put a lot of thought into how we felt the internship program could be developed, you know, in the way that it would suit the schools and the teachers and the interns best. (Matt)

The seconded teachers' perception of their role in the internship process is a very positive one. They believe strongly that they have something very special to offer in the form of skills and competencies that the university-based professor/supervisors and the cooperative teachers, may not be able to offer. They believe they bring a unique perspective from their teaching experiences in the school system. The following quotes from seconded teachers typically represent this type of perception:

> I think the very nature of the two experiences [teacher vs. professor] makes the difference and I'm going to say that my view is that the active teacher who is seconded, to be a supervisor might have the edge over the university professor who hasn't been in the classroom situation for some time. I feel very strongly about that as a matter of fact. (David)

> These [seconded teachers] are the people who know where it is at. These are people who are not at arm's lengths from the education of children in whatever level you're talking about. They haven't been distanced from it and therefore they know exactly what you talk about when you talk about the stress of having somebody in your class who may be a behaviour problem. (Barbara)

The seconded teachers believe their relationship with school-based cooperating teachers can be more objective than the relationship between cooperating teacher, university professors and interns. They feel their ability to be objective enables them to reduce the tension that often exists between cooperating teachers and teacher interns.

The seconded teachers also attach some degree of status, prestige and pride to the position of seconded teacher as university supervisor. They seem to view this position located somewhere between the cooperating teachers who are still in the classroom and the supervisors who are structurally located at the university. To summarize briefly, they seem to believe they were selected as internship supervisors because in the eyes of their school boards they were the most effective teachers, a "model" or "master teacher," in terms of personal and professional abilities and competencies. They were the best-suited teachers to carry out the role of supervising interns at the university level. They also felt ethically responsible to correct what they perceive to be weakness in the pre-service programs offered to students in the university. Here are some statements that typify this perception:

> It's nice to be recognized for your contribution and they can look at you and say you're good, you're a very effective teacher. You've been involved in many aspects with our board and here's a little bonus for you. We're giving you four months in at the university. Again the staff looks at it as status to know that you're going in there, you've gotten this opportunity, you're working at the university. All these things mean a lot to other people on staff. (Pam)

The seconded teachers envision a valuable role for experienced teachers in the internship program. They believe recent initiatives surrounding current educational reform can provide new windows of opportunity for creating new roles for school-based experienced teachers. However, throughout the discussions, they addressed a number of issues that underscore the complexity of their involvement in the internship program as supervisors. Regarding the selection and acceptability of seconded teachers as university supervisors, the following claim was made. "I'm going to assume that when a teacher is sec

onded to become supervisor of interns that he has been selected very carefully and that he's reputable" (Dan).

> I would suggest that if you ask six people for a description of a good teacher you might get six different answers. And then I might suggest that the good teacher might fit into all six categories. He might be all six of these. I'm not sure if you know when you ask an individual what does a good teacher do, if they listed down all of the characteristics of the good teacher. If each of the staff members and let's suppose

there were ten staff members involved, and if they listed all of the characteristics of good teacher then I believe you would have some common things but if you asked them for one or two, you might find that they'd all give you different ones. (Debbie)

Some seconded teachers envisioned that their experience gained through the role of seconded teachers would have an impact on their future practice and ongoing professional development. These comments reflect some of their ideas in this regard:

I'm going back to a classroom when I finish this job in April, and I'm going back with some good ideas. I'm going back with some new combinations of pieces of literature that I have never put together before, some new insights. I think I'm going back a little bit revived. I believe, too, when the school board selected me, or when my principal selected me, they may have had that in mind. It's not exactly been retraining, but I think it has been a source of revitalization and so it's been good for me, and I hope it's been good for my interns. (Jo).

It is plain to see what part Henry Giroux had in developing this pedagogy. In many ways we have mapped a journey where we started off reading Henry Giroux in a way that would enliven our own learning, and that in turn seeped into our teaching, which is often reflected in what our students and colleagues think, say and write.

Bibliography

Darling-Hammond, L., Bransford, J. (2005). Preparing teachers for a changing world. San Francisco: Jossey-Bass.

Doyle, C. (1993). Raising curtains on education. Westport, Conn.: Bergin & Garvey.

Doyle, C., Kennedy, W. (1995). Perceptions of internship education. *The Australian Journal of Teaching Practice*. Monash University Press. Vol. 15, 40–54.

Giroux, H. A. (1981). Ideology, culture and the process of schooling. Philadelphia: Temple University Press; London: Farmer Press.

—(1983). Theory and resistance in education: a pedagogy for the opposition. London: Heinemann Educational Book.

Giroux, H. A., Purpel, D. (1983). The hidden curriculum and moral education: deception or discovery? Berkeley, Calif.: McCutchan Pub. Corp.

Giroux, H. A. (1988a). Teachers as intellectuals: toward a critical pedagogy of learning. London: Bergin & Garvey.

—(1988b). Schooling for democracy: critical pedagogy in the modern age. London: Routledge.

—(1988c). Schooling and the struggle for public life: democracy's promise and education's challenge. Boulder, Colo.: Paradigm Publishers.

Giroux, H. A., Simon, R. I. (1989). Popular culture, schooling, and everyday life. Granby, Mass.: Bergin & Garvey.

Giroux, H., & McLaren, P. (1989). Critical pedagogy, the state, and cultural struggle. Albany: State University of New York Press.

Giroux, H. A. (Ed). (1991). Postmodernism, feminism, and cultural politics: redrawing educational boundaries. Albany: State University of New York Press.

Giroux, H. A., Aronowitz, S. (1991). Postmodern Education: politics, culture, and social criticism. Minneapolis: University of Minnesota Press.

Giroux, H. A. (1993a). Living dangerously: multiculturalism and the politics of difference. New York: Peter Lang Publishing, Inc.

—(1993b). Border crossings: cultural workers and the politics of education. New York: Routledge.

Giroux, H. A., McLaren, P. (Eds.). (1994). Between borders: pedagogy and the politics of cultural studies. New York, London: Routledge.

Giroux, H. A., Aronowitz, S. (1994). Education still under siege. Westport, Conn.: Bergin & Garvey.

Giroux, H. A. (1994). Disturbing pleasures: learning popular culture. New York: Routledge.

—(1996). Fugitive cultures: race, violence, and youth. New York, London: Routledge.

Giroux, H. A., Larkshear, C., McLaren, P., Peters, M. (Eds.). (1996). Counternarratives: cultural studies and critical pedagogies in postmodern spaces. New York: Routledge.

Giroux, H. A. (1997a). Pedagogy and the politics of hope: theory, culture, and schooling: a critical reader. Boulder, Colo.: Westview Press.

—(1997b). Channel surfing: race talk and the destruction of today's youth. Toronto, Ont.: Canadian Scholars Press.

Giroux, H. A., Shannon, P. (1997). Education and cultural studies: toward a performative practice. New York: Routledge.

Giroux, H. A. (2000). Impure acts: the practical politics of cultural studies. New York: Routledge.

Giroux, H. A., Myrsiades, K. (Eds.). (2001). Beyond the corporate university: culture and pedagogy in the new millennium. Lanham Md.: Rowman & Littlefield.

Giroux, H. A. (2003a). The abandoned generation: democracy beyond the culture of fear. New York: Palgrave Macmillan.

—(2003b). Public spaces, private lives: beyond the culture of cynicism. Lanham: Rowman & Littlefield Publishers: Distributed by National Book Network.

—(2003c). Public time and educated hope: educational leadership and the war against youth. Retrieved September 18 from The Initiative Anthology database.

—(2004). The terror of neoliberalism. Boulder Colo.: Paradigm Publishers; Aurora, Ont.: Garamond Press.

Giroux, H. A., Giroux, S. (2004). Take back higher education: race, youth, and the crisis of democracy in the post-civil rights era. New York: Palgrave Macmillan.

Giroux, H. A. (2nd ed.). (2005a). Border crossings: cultural workers and the politics of education. New York : Routledge.

—(2nd ed.). (2005b). Schooling and the struggle for public life: democracy's promise and education's challenge. Boulder, Colo.: Paradigm Publishers.

Kennedy, W., Doyle, C., Rose, A., Singh, A. Teaching internship: a reflective practice, in Hoz, Ron & Moshe Silberstein. (Eds.) (1993). Partnerships of schools and institutions of higher education in teacher development. Isreal: Be-Gurion University of the Negev Press.

McLaren, P., Giarelli, J. (1995). Critical theory and educational research. Albany: State University of New York Press.

An Educator's Reflections on the Crisis in Education and Democracy in the US: An Interview with Henry A. Giroux, Michael Alexander Pozo, www.dissidentvoice.org, September 25, 2004.

Schon, D. (1983). The reflective practitioner. New York: Basic Books.

—(1987). Educating the reflective practitioner. San Francisco: Jossey-Bass.

Simon, R.0 (1992). Teaching against the grain: texts for a pedagogy of possibility. New York: Bergin and Garvey.

Singh, A., Doyle, C., Rose, A., Kennedy, W. "Reflective Internship and the Phobia of Classroom Management." Australian Journal of Education 41.2, (1997): 105–118.

Singh, A., Hamnett, M., Porter, D., Kumar, K. (1984). Ethics, politics, and international social science research: from critique to praxis. Honolulu: University of Hawaii Press.

Singh, A., Doyle, C., Kennedy, W., Rose, A., Ludlow, K. (2001). Teacher training: a reflective perspective. New Delhi: Kanishka Publishers, Distributors.

Singh, A. (2001). Classroom management: a reflective perspective. New Delhi: Kanishka Publishers, Distributors.

Index

TEACHING

•CONTEMPORARY•

SCHOLARS

Joe L. Kincheloe & Shirley R. Steinberg
General Editors

This innovative series addresses the pedagogies and thoughts of influential contemporary scholars in diverse fields. Focusing on scholars who have challenged the "normal science," the dominant frameworks of particular disciplines, *Teaching Contemporary Scholars* highlights the work of those who have profoundly influenced the direction of academic work. In a era of great change, this series focuses on the bold thinkers who provide not only insight into the nature of the change but where we should be going in light of the new conditions. Not a festschrift, not a re-interpretation of past work, these books allow the reader a deeper, yet accessible conceptual framework in which to negotiate and expand the work of important thinkers.

For additional information about this series or for the submission of manuscripts, please contact:

> Joe L. Kincheloe & Shirley R. Steinberg
> c/o Peter Lang Publishing, Inc.
> 29 Broadway, 18th floor
> New York, New York 10006

To order other books in this series, please contact our Customer Service Department:

> (800) 770-LANG (within the U.S.)
> (212) 647-7706 (outside the U.S.)
> (212) 647-7707 FAX

Or browse online by series:

> WWW.PETERLANG.COM